# The Heart of the Healer

### Edited By
### Dawson Church and Dr. Alan Sherr

Aslan
PUBLISHING

New York, New York
Mickleton, England

Published by

**ASLAN PUBLISHING**
310 Blue Ridge Drive
BOULDER CREEK, CA 95006
**(408) 338-7504**

Mickleton House
Mickleton, Gloucestershire GL55 6RY
England

Library of Congress Catalog Card Number: 87-71789

The Heart of the Healer
Bibliography: p.
1. Medical personnel and patient. 2. Healing –
Psychological aspects. 3. Holistic Medicine. I. Church,
Dawson, 1956-     . II. Sherr, Alan, 1954-
R727.3.H42   1987     610.69       87-17480
ISBN 0-944031-12-9  (pbk.)

© 1987, Aslan Publishing

The chapters by Norman Cousins, Larry Dossey, Francis MacNutt and Bernard Siegel
have been reprinted from other sources by permission of the original publishers.

Cover Illustration by Chuck Waltmire
Book Production by Brenda Plowman
Set in Times Roman typeface
Printed in U.S.A. by Mitchell-Shear
10 9 8 7 6 5 4 3
First Edition

This book is dedicated to Dr. Bill Bahan,
founder of the Whole Health Institute.
His powerful spirit of welcome and thankfulness
inspired thousands of healing professionals all over the
world, who called him "friend," to rise up to
a new vision of the healer's true position:
an emissary of life, to the individual
and the whole.

# Acknowledgments:

The Editors wish to publicly thank the following individuals and organizations for their assistance in bringing this book about: for assistance in producing the text: Apple Computer, Guy Daniels, Dawson Design, the Huntington Chiropractic and Wellness Center, and MicroComputer Publishing Center and David Webb; for marketing advice and assistance: Barbara Somerfield and Aurora Press, Peter Garrett and Foundation House Publications, Dan Poynter, Publishers Marketing Association, Astrid Seeburg, and Erroll Sowers and Stillpoint Publishing; and for inspiration and nurture of the ideas: Patch Adams, M.D., Sherrill Akyol, the Ark Communications Institute, Lord Exeter, Steve Frankel and the Garden City Emissary Center, the International Center for Integrative Studies, Larry Kranz, M.D., Karen Larson, Dean James Parks Morton of the Cathedral Church of St. John the Divine, N. Y. Public Library, Brenda Plowman, Prof. Janis Roze, Lisinka Ulatowska, Kate and Simon Warwick-Smith, Bryant Wedge, M.D., and Kate Zahorsky.

Credit for the photograph of Prince Charles goes to British Information Services; for Victor Krivorotov to Nancy Caudle; for illustrations in Susanna Davis chapter to Lin Fell.

# Contents

# *Preface*

Lunches are dangerous things, especially when creative people get together! "You never know what might happen," as the bishop said to the actress. Alan Sherr and I accidentally sat down together at one, and this book is the result, beginning life as some scrawled notes on the back of a bridge toll receipt.

We had both long been active in the Whole Health Institute, an international network of healing professionals and laymen. Over the years it has been a gathering place for many in the healing arts seeking a healing model that transcends mere technique. The Institute was founded by the late Bill Bahan, D.C, whose lectures and personal representation of a healing atmosphere vividly rekindled the passion of healing in thousands of health professionals as he tirelessly travelled the world.

The theme then emerging for the 1987 Whole Health Institute convention was "The Heart of Healing." This concept inspired us to undertake to speak to some remarkable healers about their personal experience and inner journeys. Initially we saw this work merely as a compilation of the ideas of some of the people who would be presenters at the conference. However, as the project progressed, it became evident that we had touched a deep, resounding chord in the hearts of health professionals, and the scope of the work grew as a larger number of other authors responded with rich and powerful submissions.

Acknowledging our connection with the great new paradigm of healing that is emerging in human consciousness, the editors and publisher felt it fitting that all royalties from the sale of this book go to benefit the Whole Health Institute. None of the authors or editors has received any financial remuneration for their contribution to the book. The privilege of serving the heart of the healer is recompense enough.

The nurturing heart of the true healer, with all its tenderness, giving, sensitivity and caring innocence, is a precious commodity. We hope that this book will touch it, acknowledge it, and help sustain it.

*— Dawson Church*

# *Introduction*

The proliferation of approaches to healing and medicine today, with its smorgasbord of treatments, from the exotic and unproven, to long-standing and well-understood procedures, presents the patient with a bewildering array of choices. Yet more crucial, we believe, than the method of treatment adopted, are the inner workings of doctor and patient. Factors like attitude, belief, faith, stillness, and so forth, are unquantifiable and perhaps unmeasurable, yet they have an enormous relevance to the healing process. They can reinforce the efficacy of a particular treatment or doom it.

In our Western obsession with 'objectivity,' with its em - phasis on repeatable experimentation, a study of healing is thought to be tainted if any of these factors creep in. Yet as these chapters so eloquently show, behind the therapy is the therapist, and behind the disease is the patient. Looking at the disease and the therapy, rather than the healer and the healed, robs us of our very humanity. It renders medicine an impassive, inerrant, uncontrollable monument, on a plane removed from the uncer - tainties and unpredictability of everyday human life.

But what of science...the science of healing? It has a vital place, but that place is in the context of healing as an art. The painter wields brush and paints to give voice to the creative urges within. Yet the brush is the end-product of a long technological and manufacturing process. So are the paints. What the artist creates with them, however, far transcends their value as technology and chemical formulae. It is the living expression of a set of inner values.

So also in healing. The great healer must master his technique, as must the great painter. But the true healer wields technique as a master – a master of the art of healing – never becoming so lost in the mechanism of science that he forgets the essence of healing as an art.

*The Heart of the Healer* thus contains chapters by authors who have chosen to express their art through several different techniques. Little consideration was given to the technical tradition out of which they sprang. The editors sought to let contributors tell their own stories, from their own perspectives, without confining the inquiry to an ideological straightjacket; hence the diversity of some of the views expressed. Some are M.D.'s or chiropractors, others are psychologists, mystics or priests. Yet there is a remarkable underlying unity that springs from what each of them have to say.

Some great common themes emerge. Perhaps the most striking of these is the often reported experience of entering a state in which there is no perception of healer and healed, only of oneness. This is the inner state from which healing proceeds, an 'inner ground of healing' characterized by stillness, peace, and a sense of the infinite wellness of all things.

Seeking the core of what 'makes' a healer leads the inquirer beyond any favored therapeutic approach. It involves a fearless personal evaluation of one's inner state, to what it means to be 'standing in the place of healing.' From this stance everything one touches is imbued with life; everyone one treats stands within the compass of one's own atmosphere.

In the 'strictly scientific' approach to medicine that came into its own in the nineteenth century, pioneered by visionary surgeons like Ignaz Semmelweiss and James Lister, the fathers of antiseptic sterilization, the sphere of the responsible healer unintentionally became more and more confined to the definition and treatment of ill conditions of the human body.

With Freud, and the development of psychoanalysis and its progeny, even the elusive mind became subject to systematic analysis, definition and prescribable treatment. By the middle of the twentieth century, the medical profession was convinced that every something called a 'disease' had something called a 'cure', and that the irrevocable march of research would eventually place in the healer's hands the tools to eradicate virtually every human ailment.

This myth was seriously dented by the intractability of diseases like cancer, in which the nature of the human being as a circular continuum of body, mind and heart, or rather the ancient Greek idea of 'body, soul and spirit' is evident. Diseases of the body are not confined to the body. They may be caused by the mind or heart, and have real and observable effects upon the soul and spirit. Indeed, the division of the human being into component parts is for the convenience of discussion only: real human beings are indivisible. Wellness or illness in one part of the system affects the whole. Illness cannot be successfully treated in one part of the organism only.

Here the realms of anatomy, psychology, and spirituality fuse, and the idea of 'holistic' treatment emerges: respect for the integrity of the whole system, rather than fragmented attention to symptoms. This synthesis has come to make sense to more and more medical practitioners, who can breathe a sigh of relief at not having to judge their performance by their success at temporarily manipulating a bit of the whole. Healers are not mechanics, driving the patient's body to surgery or the medicine cabinet, replacing a faulty distributor cap or doing an oil change, and sending them, 'healed,' on their way. Rather, honoring both the 'human' and the 'being' aspects of the human being, we find ways to become sensitive to the implicit order and rhythms of life, and facilitate their unobstructed expression through those we serve.

In doing this we reclaim our links to the oldest forms of healing. The ancient tribal shaman used prayer and supplications to the gods, herbal remedies (as many of our modern "miracle" drugs are derivatives of substances extracted from plants) and the support of family and society. Drugs and surgery have also long been potent arrows in the quiver of the medical profession, and only in the last century has the peculiar practice of limiting medical authenticity to these two tools become widespread.

The modern and truly holistic healer sees no need to restrict himself to this partial approach. If healing is the desired goal, then what promotes healing? Does prayer promote healing? Then let doctor and patient pray together. Is psychotherapy effective? Let it take its place in the lexicon of legitimate treatments. Will the warmth and closeness of good friends be an effective tonic? Then encourage their presence. Do drugs and surgery have their unique value? Then have them available as tools for appropriate use. All these things are the province of the healer, and to the degree that a healer's preconceptions or pet theories preclude the use of one or more of these, to that degree are that healer's patients impoverished, and denied the resources of the fullness of life to effect healing. This is as true of those who practice allopathic, or disease-centered medicine, as those who go overboard on 'alternative' approaches that seek to deny the remarkable advances of twentieth century medicine in the fields of drugs and surgery.

Most of those who make professional careers in the healing arts start with a burning desire to enrich the lives of others by offering them the gifts of freedom from pain, relief from anxiety and suffering, and the blessings of wellness. Healers are healers because they want to give. Yet all kinds of things get in the way – the indoctrination of schooling, the grind of getting a practice started, the healer-patient routines that develop, the pressure of peer evaluation, personal desires, such as getting ahead and making money, the fear of malpractice lawsuits. All these things become a shroud covering up that beautiful original impulse –

the magic that springs from the heart of the healer. The passionate flame of service does not endure; burnout ensues.

Healing starts with life. When we cut a finger and place a band-aid over the wound, is it the band-aid that causes the healing? Of course not! The natural processes of life operating through that particular human body provide the healing. And that is the thing with which the effective healer is aligned. When the healer and healee both recognize themselves to be part of the whole process, that process comes to a specific focus in that situation, and healing is a natural manifestation.

The interest of the new healer is life, and what it is that leads to a greater abundance of life. Gone is the fixation upon disease, which is merely the result of the blockage of that innate energy. The vision is instead on what makes people well; what keeps people well. The healer who makes it his first business to align himself with that creative process is truly a gift to his patients, as well as a medium for the release of an increasing quantum of the balm of life so desperately required in an ailing world. The new healer, the complete healer, the truly 'modern' healer, fuses in his practice enduring ancient truth with modern technique. It does not matter whether the new healer chooses to equip his therapeutic toolbag with surgery, chiropractic, or herbology.

What does matter is the heart of the healer, and whether or not it is imprisoned within the structured confines of a favored method, its energy channeled into defending its prison. When released, it may blossom into fulfillment with its first love: the love of serving the whole of life.

# Reclaiming the Spirit of Healing

## by His Royal Highness
## Charles, Prince of Wales

I have often thought that one of the less attractive traits of various professional bodies and institutions is the deeply in - grained suspicion and outright hostility which can exist towards anything unorthodox or unconventional. I suppose it is inevit - able that something which is different should arouse strong feelings on the part of the majority whose conventional wisdom is being challenged or, in a more social sense, whose way of life and customs are being insulted by something rather alien.

I suppose, too, that human nature is such that we are fre - quently prevented from seeing that what is taken for today's unorthodoxy is probably going to be tomorrow's convention. Perhaps we just have to accept it is God's will that the unorthodox individual is doomed to years of frustration, ridicule and failure in order to act out his role in the scheme of things, until his day arrives and mankind is ready to receive his message: a message which he probably finds hard to explain, but which he knows comes from a far deeper source than conscious thought.

*His Royal Highness, Charles, the Prince of Wales is heir apparent to the English throne. Educated in England and Australia, he has served in the Royal Navy and Royal Air Force. He has made many official and unofficial visits to other countries, as well as familiarizing himself with different aspects of British life. He has a great diversity of interests, including education, nature conservation, disabilities, music, history, flying and complementary medicine. He is married to Lady Diana Spencer. They have two children, William and Henry. This chapter is based on a speech given to the British Medical Association on the 14th of December 1982.*

The renowned sixteenth century healer, Paracelsus, was just such an individual. He is probably remembered more for his fight against orthodoxy than for his achievements in the medical field. As a result of his unorthodox approach to medicine in his time he was equated with the damnable Dr. Faustus.

Of the barbers, surgeons and pharmacists, he complained that "they begrudge the honour I won healing Princes and noble - men and they say my powers come from the devil." And yet in his day and age he was criticizing abuses among pharmacists and attacking the quack remedies — vipers' blood, "mummy" powder, unicorn horn and so on.

In 1527, by an act of which I am sure today's younger doctors would be proud, he burnt the famous textbook of medieval medicine, the *Canon of Avicenna,* which became a symbol of rebellion against pedantry and unthinking acceptance of ancient doctrines.

But what kind of man was Paracelsus? A charlatan or a gifted healer? In my view he was far from being a charlatan. We could do worse than to look again briefly at the principles he so desperately believed in, for they have a message for our time: a time when science has tended to become estranged from nature, and that is the moment when we should remember Paracelsus.

Above all, he maintained that there were four pillars on which the whole art of healing rested. The first was philosophy; the second astronomy (or what we might call psychology): the third alchemy (or bio-chemistry), and the fourth, virtue (in other words the professional skill of a doctor). He then went on to outline the basic qualifications for a doctor: "Like each plant and metallic remedy the doctor, too, must have a specific virtue. He must be intimate with nature. He must have the intuition which is necessary to understand the patient, his body, his disease. He must have the 'feel' and the 'touch' which make it possible for him to be in sympathetic communication with the patient's spirits."

Paracelsus believed that the *good* doctor's therapeutic success largely depends on his ability to inspire the patient with confidence and to mobilize his will to health. By the way, he also recommended chastity and fasting to heighten diagnostic sensitiveness and to intensify one's hypnotic power.

I know that there are a considerable number of doctors who operate by these kinds of basic principles, because several have written to me, but nevertheless the modern science of medicine still tends to be based, as George Engel writes, "...on the notion of the body as a machine, of disease as the consequence of breakdown of the machine, and of the doctor's task as the repairer of the machine." By concentrating on smaller and smaller fragments of the body, modern medicine perhaps loses sight of the patient as a whole human being, and by reducing health to mechanical functioning it is no longer able to deal with the phenomenon of healing.

And here I come back to my original point. The term "healer" is viewed with suspicion and the concepts of health and healing are probably not generally discussed in medical schools. But to reincorporate the notion of healing into the practice of medicine does not necessarily mean that medical science will have to be less scientific.

Through the centuries healing has been practiced by folk-healers who are guided by a traditional wisdom that sees illness as a disorder of the whole person, involving not only the patient's body, but also his mind, his self-image, his dependence on the physical and social environment, as well as his relation to the cosmos.

Paracelsus constantly repeated the old adage that "Nature heals, the doctor nurses" – and it is well to remember that these sorts of healers still treat the majority of patients throughout the world. Some of them, in the form of black Christian bishops in Africa, are subjected to the most appalling kind of misinformed abuse and censure, which so characterized the worst elements of missionary activity among populations whose childlike accep - tance of the symbols of life and of nature is one of their most endearing and vital qualities.

I would suggest that the whole imposing edifice of modern medicine, for all its breathtaking successes is, like the celebrated Tower of Pisa, slightly off balance. No one could be stupid enough to deny the enormous benefits which the advances of medical science in this century have conferred upon us all. To take only one example – penicillin administered in a case of infective heart disease leads to survival in an illness otherwise uniformly fatal. Anyone who has had this kind of experience is likely to be a powerful supporter of modern methods in medicine, but nevertheless the fact remains that contemporary medicine as a whole tends to be fascinated by the objective, statistical, computerized approach to the healing of the sick.

If disease is regarded as an objective problem, isolated from all personal factors, then surgery plus more and more powerful drugs must be the answer. Already the cost of drugs supplied to patients by the British National Health Service alone is well over three and a half billion dollars a year. It is frightening how dependent upon drugs we are all becoming and how easy it is for doctors to prescribe them as the universal panacea for our ills. Wonderful as many of them are, it should still be more widely stressed by doctors that the health of human beings is so often determined by their behavior, their food and the nature of their environment.

The last word on this subject remains with Paracelsus, whose name should be synonymous with the common health. He hoped to show, above all, that the "light of Nature" was in the hearts of men, not in books. With all the conviction of a man who follows his inner voice he made a desperate supplication that "would we humans knew our hearts in truth, nothing on earth would be impossible for us."

# The Healing Power of Innocence

## by Michael, Lord Burghley

As we look out at the world it appears that there are many problems facing us. No purpose is served by becoming preoccupied with what seems to be wrong, as has been a common habit. On the other hand, there is nothing amiss with observing what seems to be taking place and to have a realistic view of that. Such matters can be taken lightly if there is some sense that behind all the difficulty and all the anxiety is another possibility – the actual availability of life and health and wholeness.

There has been much publicity about AIDS, the current immune system problem. Fearful race memories linger of the Black Death, which carried away a large proportion of the European population. The U.S. Surgeon General has warned about how widespread the disease could become in the U.S. among the heterosexual population in the next ten or twelve years. Valerie Andrews said some things in a perceptive article in the *Tarrytown Letter* that bear on all this:

"AIDS has come to us at a time when our traditional bonds are breaking down – ties to family, friends,

*Born in Canada, Michael Burghley was educated in England. He is part of the Cecil family, which has long been prominent in British public life. He is heir to the title of Marquess of Exeter and a seat in the House of Lords. As international director of the Emissary Society, he travels extensively, meeting with many on the leading edge of world affairs. His commitment to facilitating integrative change in society embraces all areas in which he is active: business management, conferences and seminars and coordination of Emissary communities. He lives in 100 Mile House, British Columbia with his wife, Nancy, and their family. He is the author of* The Rising Tide of Change. *(see pg. 240)* community. This disease came in on the heels of the Sexual Revolution and for a long time we have been living on intimacy without trust. Through AIDS the body is protesting and forcing us to look into the heart of our relationships."[1]

It would appear that our civilization has lost the sense of the sacred and perhaps, through this disease in particular, the fact is emphasized. The above article compares the gay community to the canaries in the mine shaft for all of society. These little birds were taken down the mines to warn miners of the buildup of lethal coal gas. If a bird died, the miners knew they had to get out of the shaft – fast! The gay community represents a parti - cular kind of anxiety and isolation. But this sense of isolation, of being away from one's roots, in the deepest sense of the word, is all-pervasive, and not just in North America.

An urge is moving in a lot of people to find the inner spiritual self. The Christian Science Monitor has this to say about the Soviets:

"The post-Brezhnev era has revealed what leading Soviet writers say is a spiritual crisis in Soviet society. The pages of the country's literary journals have been flooded with writing depicting the moral degradation of the Soviet people almost 70 years after the Russian Revolution. 'What happened to us?' asked Victor Astafyev, a widely published writer, in a recent article. 'Who hurled us into the depths of evil and misfortune, and why? Who extinguished the light of goodness in our soul ? Who blew out the lamp of our conscience, toppled it into a dark, deep pit in which we are groping, trying to find the bottom, a support and some kind of guiding light to the future?'"[2]

This evidently is representative of much Soviet thought right now, and in some the urge is to return to the Russian Orthodox Church. Enough time seems to have passed for Russians to have forgotten that one of the reasons for the Russian revolution was exasperation with the Church! So the world-wide urge isn't really for religiosity, but for spirituality: for a return to the sense of the sacred – in particular, (thinking of the spiritual implications of AIDS) a return insofar as our bodies are concerned.

From the way they treat their physical bodies, people demonstrate a general attitude that this physical mechanism is of little value. It is perceived to be there merely for our mani - pulation to satisfy our emotional and mental compulsions in any way that we can arrange it. There is a loss of the sense of the sacred apparent when physical matter is mistreated, as though it didn't mean much. Yet we have had ample proof that whatever occurs in our own immediate experience is projected into the world-at-large. The sad state of the world environment is like a large mirror, reflecting the individual's loss of sacredness.

There has been much news recently about what has hap - pened to the ozone layer of the earth's atmosphere. This layer has been protecting the biosphere from ultraviolet solar radia - tion. A large "hole" has appeared over Antarctica and another one is growing over the North Pole. This is the result apparently of various man-made chemicals, especially freon gas. And now, once again, technology and science is being used to find alternative ways of running our air-conditioning systems.

When we are in this position of isolation from the whole and have lost our sense of sacredness, of the intricate way in which life's design fits together, all our bright ideas end up as cata - strophes. I suspect that whatever solution is found to halt the further deterioration of the ozone layer will have its own

17

repercussions. That is invariably the case until there is a return to a respect for how life really works.

The innate intuitive sense of how life really works is available to us all. Yet I would underline that it simply is not possible to have intuition that is accurate to the way life is working when our intuitive responses are buried by our sophis - tication. Before they can re-emerge, we must detoxify ourselves from the control of that sophistication.

Early American and other aboriginal peoples had a natural and innate relatedness to the way things work. They didn't have to think too much about it. Today all of us have too much thought, and that thought invariably comes on the heels of emotional compulsions. However, if we were simply to lay aside our conscious mental activity for the moment – plans, definitions, goals – I expect that the effects of unbridling the subconscious mind would, in its existing mixed-up state, be no improvement.

For example, one of the worthy goals we have, consciously, is to love one another. But how shall love be expressed? Who actually knows what love is? We know a lot about sentiment, we know a lot about the desire to care for people, but what is love? Those who were motivated to combat infant mortality through better health care saved many, compelled by a current of caring. Yet these children, surviving into adulthood, have produced massive population growth. Unsustainable populations in turn contribute to the degradation of the environment.

Therefore, what is the appropriate expression of love? We cannot know that until we accept a measure of *control in ourselves,* a control which springs from a spirit of humility and innocence and total openness to the larger design of life and what it would require of us in any moment. It does not spring from our minds with their habits and traditions, or from the environment, or from what somebody is telling us. Love is the power that runs the universe, the motivating impulse back of all life, and a far larger force than any colorations of human emotion.

How can that find release in us in a truly creative way? Its inherent design is symbolized so beautifully in our bodies and present in the world around us. Yet we still manage to regularly overlook it, treating it as irrelevant!

If we are to be in position to offer any spirit of healing into our larger world, then the qualities of innocence and humility must be consistently maintained. Integrity demands expressing these through mind, through heart, regardless of the fact that there may be emotional pulls of one sort or another or the invitation to mental argument. Integrity decrees that one be available to coordinate as fully as possible with the way life works. Therefore there must be humility, an openness to sense what that would mean and to let it happen. Then there is room in our hearts for genuine enfoldment of people and the ability to encourage them to move easily in the creative process. The message comes across that we can take life much more lightly, that back of all this confusion and difficulty we have generated there is an intrinsic order. Things will work the way they need to, and we need not judge *any* of it.

This is one of the biggest problems of all: we think we know how things should be. We think that there is an advantage in judging how things are. That concept creates the difficulty! If we will just stop struggling to build a satisfactory world for ourselves, let go to the fact of life's *intrinsic* order, then everything can begin to clarify. Then mind and emotions begin to come clear themselves, so that they can sense what *is* unfolding.

It need no longer be a mystery. When the human mind-emotion-body continuum comes into alignment in this way, there is an avenue for the release of an immensity of power. If this detoxification process is allowed to happen, with mind and emotions held still, in the spirit of integrity, so that the available power of love can come through, then we have an inevitably creative outcome.

The idea that we can set the world right by any kind of physical manipulation is short-sighted. What we have assessed as needing change is inevitably only a little fraction of a much larger whole. The real detoxification is needed inside. To accomplish that, there must be absolute humility, so that one is available, without judgment, to hear what life is indicating. Then there is space for the real magic to work.

**Notes:**
1  Valerie Andrews, *AIDS: Our First Planetary Illness,* "Tarrytown Letter," January 1986.
2  Boris Rumer, *Soviet Writers Decry Loss of Spiritual Values in Society,* The Christian Science Monitor.

# Changing Fashions in Disease

## by Norman Cousins

The report of the U.S. Surgeon General for 1980 begins with the auspicious statement that the American people have never been healthier. As prime evidence, the report cites the fact that life expectancy for both sexes is now in the mid-70's. Four diseases that at the turn of the century were major killers – diphtheria, tuberculosis, gastroenteritis, and poliomyelitis – have been brought under control. In 1980, the combined death toll in the United States from those four diseases was 10,000. If the death rate in 1900 had persisted, the death toll in 1978 would have been 875,000. Even some forms of cancer are now on the decrease – cancer of the stomach, for example. The rising curve in the incidence of heart disease has flattened out.

This improvement in the nation's health is attributable to many factors, not the least among them the continuing develop - ment of advanced medical technology. Within little more than two decades, new techniques have been devised both to diag - nose otherwise elusive cases and to treat cases of extraordinary complexity. The usefulness of transistors in detecting subtle changes in internal chemistry, or to regulate heartbeat; the efficiency of laser beams in intricate surgery without the hazards

*Norman Cousins, Ph.D. edited the* Saturday Review *for 35 years, and is now a professor in the School of Medicine at the University of California, Los Angeles. He holds honorary degrees from 53 colleges and universities. His achievements in the fields of journalism, literature, medicine, diplomacy and public policy have been recognized through numerous awards bestowed by nations and institutions, including the United Nations Peace Medal and the American Peace Award. He is the author of twenty books, including* Anatomy of an Illness, The Healing Heart, *and* Albert Schweitzer's Mission.. *(see pg. 240)*
This chapter is reprinted from *The Healing Heart*, published by W.W. Norton and Co., Inc., New York, and is reprinted by permission of the publisher, W.W. Norton and Co., Inc.

of blood loss; the help furnished by computers in dealing with shock; the remarkable contributions made by science and technology to organ transplants; the prodigious forward leap represented by computerized tomography; the availability not just of radioactive tracers, but of sound and echoes to provide basic information; cardiopulmonary bypass machines; high-voltage radiation; kidney-dialysis devices; blood-gas analyses – all these are only a few examples of the rapidly enlarging role of machines and chemistry in the war against disease.

But inevitable questions arise. What effect does advanced medical technology have on the physician-patient relationship? Indeed, how do the new techniques affect the practice of medicine? And how does the public at large react to its own new role, one created for it by the rapid progress made by medical technology?

Perhaps the most tangible impact of the new developments are the emergence of a new breed of physicians who are uncomfortable with the notion that medicine can be practiced out of a little black bag. Indeed, the reluctance to make house calls may be a reflection more of the dependence on headquartered high technology than of time limitations alone. No one can doubt the vast extension of the physician's competence represented by scientific instrumentation. The doubt rather is whether science has cut into the physician's art – a vital ingredient in the treatment of humans. The practice of medicine, as it has been emphasized over the centuries by almost every great medical teacher – from Hippocrates to Holmes, from Galen to Cannon, from Castiglione to Osler – calls first of all for a deeply human response by the physician to the cry of the patient for help. In the overwhelming majority of cases, as Franz Ingelfinger, the late and much-loved editor of the *New England Journal of Medicine* pointed out, what patients need most of all is assurance that their own healing systems are beautifully designed to handle most of their complaints. The physician who understands the importance of sitting at a bedside, even though his presence may actually be in the nature of a placebo, is tending to a prevalent and therefore, quintessential need.

"If the critical-care specialist," writes James J. Strain in *Critical Care Medicine,* for January-February 1978, "is to provide adequate medical and psychological care for his patient, he must understand the nature of the psychological stresses the patient is experiencing, and be able to enhance the patient's ability to adapt his situation."

"Technological knowledge," wrote Malcolm C. Todd in *Medical Instrumentation,* May-June 1977, "must be supple - mented by a broad understanding of man's nature, lest limited points of view generate an oversimplified formula of action." It should be no surprise, therefore, that resistance by many patients to medical technology is not unnatural and ought not to be regarded by the reasonable physician as a challenge to his authority. Such a situation offers the physician an opportunity for adroit and compassionate negotiations.

It is likely that the chances of a patient's opposing or resenting medical technology are in direct proportion to the physician's distance from the scene. People feel secure in the presence of their doctors. It is only when the patients are dispatched to other places and are deprived of direct contact with or access to their own physician that they tend to become uneasy. And the more removed they are from the main source of their security, the more apprehensive they become.

The wise physician, therefore, makes a careful estimate of the mind-set and emotional needs of the patient. He creates the mood of confidence for the encounter with modern technology. He explains that he will not attach sovereign importance to the results. He doesn't abandon the patient to a device if he possibly can help it. The wise physician understands, too, that the results of the test do not necessarily forecast the response of the patient under normal conditions. My own experiences indicate that a patient's biochemistry may respond differently to challenge according to emotional and physical circumstances.

The more exotic and sophisticated the technology, the greater the likelihood that patients will feel diminished or apprehensive. The physician who cannot afford the time to stay close to the patient during this experience had better find effective equi - valents, for the ultimate impact of those tests can be harmful psychologically and therefore physiologically. Patients cannot be blamed for retreating from encounters they find distasteful or upsetting. The argument that the precedures are necessary for the patient's own good misses the point, for the source of the patient's disquiet may not be the procedure itself so much as the climate or the context in which it occurs. The absence of human warmth during those experiences can figure larger in the reactions of patients than the vaunted value of the tests.

In recent years, patients have become far more knowledge - able than they used to be about diagnostic procedures. The steady rise in the educational level of the general population is reflected in a higher level of awareness about the hazards of medical technology. The press coverage of material appearing in medical journals is certainly a factor in the reluctance of many people to accept uncritically a wide number of technological diagnostic procedures. By this time, for example, people are generally aware that the use of x-ray examinations in the past was far too promiscuous. The testimony of medical experts themselves on this matter has registered in the public mind. People compare the reassuring statements made by physicians about x-ray examinations only a decade or two ago with what is now known about the hazards of radiology. They have become aware that the effects of such exposures are cumulative; and they tend to lose confidence in physicians who routinely recommend such tests without first ascertaining the extent of previous exposures.

The value of the new technology is not absolute. It has to be measured alongside its inherent dangers. For example, the barium that is not completely eliminated from the x-ray GI series can lead to intestinal obstruction. Mammograms can carry the risk of provoking the very irregularity of cell growth they seek to detect.

The routine use of such medical technology in regular check-ups calls for serious reconsideration. It is manifestly true that the equipment can often pick up indications long before they announce themselves in symptoms. But it is equally true that the hazards associated with such tests can create health problems of their own.

The serious question arising from the comprehensive use of medical technology in regular check-ups is whether we have gone too far in persuading people to see their physicians at yearly intervals. It would be interesting to compare the number of persons who have become seriously ill in the absence of such regular examinations with the number of those who have been disadvantaged by the widespread use of medical technology as a standard feature of the annual check-ups.

There is also the matter of expense. Someone has to pay for the lavish and almost routinized use of exotic technology. The fact that the bills can be passed on in many cases to health insurance plans does not make the practice more acceptable. Now that consumerism has reached medicine, it is not to be expected that this general area will come in for increasing scrutiny.

Obviously, it would not be in the patient's own interest to forgo whatever aids technology has to offer in those cases in which such use may be absolutely necessary. Here, once again,

27

the physician has the opportunity to make such distinctions and to explain them to patients.

Finally we come to the concentrated triumph of modern medical technology. I refer, of course, to the intensive-care unit (ICU). This is where we find the grand assembly of medical invention. Technically, it does everything expected of it. It monitors the patient and picks up even the most obscure hint of biological failure. Yet the crisis atmosphere it produces contributes very little to the patient's peace of mind at a critical time. Every blip and click reminds the patient that he or she is in a precarious condition. If panic is to be avoided at all costs, the ICU can hardly be considered a bargain. It is as omnipresent as it is efficient, as forbidding as it is ingenious. Patients who are brought to the ICU are in critical condition, and they are not permitted to forget it for a single instant. Arnold Relman, in the *New England Journal of Medicine,* has written the most compelling article I have seen anywhere on the limitations and penalties of the scientific marvels of the ICU.

J.C. Holland, S. Sgroi, S. Marwit, and others reported in *Psychiatry in Medicine* in 1973 that 12.5 percent of the patients in ICU's were observed to have delirium symptoms. While it is true that delirium in varying degrees is common in patients with serious illness, the specific danger of delirium in an ICU setting is that, if the experience is prolonged, cerebral metabolism can be affected. A related study, by P.J. Tomlin, makes the point that some ICU patients exhibit the symptoms of "shell shock" victims in uninitiated clinicians, however, these psychological breakdowns appear devastating.

Does this mean that the ICU should be scuttled? Certainly not. What it means is that the patient should not be sent into this particular battleground unaccompanied and unbriefed. The presence of the primary physician at the time of arrival, his hand on the patient's shoulder, is the proper introduction to this experience. This reassuring physical and psychological precaution provides the essential backdrop for the patient's understanding of the electronic wizardry that surrounds him. The very fact that the patient's own doctor is present imparts an emotional cushioning.

In general, what applies to the ICU applies to all the other encounters with medical technology discussed in this chapter. The physician who remains close to the patient during the exercise stress test or other diagnostic procedures deprives that technology of its intimidating qualities, for it is not the technology itself but the impersonalization that frequently accompanies it that is the basis of much public resistance and apprehension.

The role of the nurse, whether with respect to the intensive-care unit or any other aspect of medical treatment, is basic and indispensable. In my own experience, I can testify that the technical knowledge of my nurses dissolved much of the for - bidding and arcane nature of the technology I encountered. Nurses are generally associated in the public mind with the need for compassionate attention. Important though this function is, it is certainly not less essential than the information a nurse is frequently able to give a patient pertaining to complicated precedures and the mysterious indicators in diagnostic techno - logy.

Medical technology has clearly justified its existence on any balance sheet of performance and problems. But the problems it presents are not minor. They affect the health and well-being of the patient. What is most significant about these problems is that they need not be unmanageable.

# The Way of Stillness

## by Janet Lang

"Descartes' famous sentence – 'I think, therefore I exist' – has led Western man to equate his identity with his mind, instead of with his whole organism... This inner fragmentation of man mirrors his view of the world 'outside.'"[1]

"From the second half of the seventeenth to the end of the nineteenth century, the mechanistic Newtonian model of the universe dominated all scientific thought. It was paralleled by the image of a monarchical God who ruled the world from above by imposing his divine law on it."[2]

By the end of the 19th century scientific thought, based on the ideas of men like Descartes and Newton, had developed a model of the universe and its underlying reality that was con - sidered nearly complete. Newton's physics and mathematics had led him to describe the universe as a great cosmic machine, set in motion by a God who was separate and unknowable. The great machine, however, could be understood by breaking it down and analyzing its component parts. From Newton's original work on gravity and motion came sophisticated mathematical

*Janet R. Lang, D.C. is a 1979 Summa Cum Laude graduate of Palmer College of Chiropractic. She is the author of the book* Understanding the Peripheral Nervous System *as well as numerous articles relating to whole person health care. A trustee of the Whole Health Institute and Editor of* Healing Currents *Magazine, Dr. Lang is a frequent lecturer on 'attunement with the creative process' and its effect on spiritual, emotional, mental and physical health. Dr. Lang has her chiropractic practice at the multiprofessional Healing Arts Clinic in Loveland, Colorado.*

formulae which could predict the motions of planets, comets and moons. By the end of the 19th century physicists could describe the celestial movements within the solar system so completely that even Newton's God seemed expendable from the formula.

In the 17th century, Descartes introduced the concept of the fundamental division between the "I" and the world. This division led science to believe that it could describe the world objectively without taking into account the human intellect doing the observing. This purely objective description of nature became the goal of science. The division of the "I" (which to Descartes meant the mind) and the world "led Western man to equate his identity with his mind, instead of his whole organism." In turn, this led science to apply a fragmented, mechanistic view of reality to human beings. The body was seen as a machine composed of parts which could be understood by de-composing them into "basic building blocks;" the mind, using its powers of logic and reason, was considered the source of ulti-mate truth. "To Descartes the material universe was a machine and nothing but a machine. There was no purpose, life, or spirituality to matter."[3]

In the West, the mechanistic and fragmented model of reality based on Newtonian physics and Cartesian philosophy pervaded the development of virtually all areas of human endeavor. The Western approach to science, technology, government, econom-ics and education all found their underlying philosophical foundations rooted in this model. Modern medicine and our traditional attitudes toward health care also sprang from these same roots.

Fritjof Capra, in his book *The Turning Point,* gives an excellent account of the philosophical evolution of modern medical thought and the present-day health care system. He writes, "The mechanistic view of the human organism has encouraged an engineering approach to health in which illness is reduced to mechanical trouble and medical therapy to technical manipulation."[4] He goes on to point out, "An important aspect of the mechanistic view of living organisms and the resulting engineering approach to health is the belief that the cure of illness requires some outside intervention by the physician... modern medicine often loses sight of the patient as a human being... In fact the question "What is health?" is generally not even addressed in medical schools, nor is there any discussion of healthy attitudes and life styles. These are considered philosophical issues that belong to the spiritual realm, outside the domain of medicine. Furthermore, medicine is supposed to be an objective science, not concerned with moral judgments."[5]

Today the pace of technological medical advances is astounding. We live in the age of organ transplants, artificial hearts, and genetic engineering. We wage complex surgical and chemical warfare on disease and the price tag for modern health care is climbing through the billions on a national scale. Yet, while the mind of Western man has been frenetically developing modern medical technology, there has been a burgeoning undercurrent of distrust and dissatisfaction with the techno - logical approach. The heretofore god-like position of the doctor is being seriously challenged as evidenced by sharply rising malpractice costs. There is an increasing interest on the part of the patient to understand and participate in his or her own health care process, and there is a demand for communication and explanation from doctors as many people will no longer blindly submit to costly and oftentimes painful testing procedures.

The undercurrent that is rising in the wake of this wave of distrust and dissatisfaction with the technological approach has given its first tentative signs of breaking surface in what is termed the "wholistic movement." The traditional health care establishment has responded with resistance and misunder - standing to this movement which challenges their mechanistic,

technical approach. The result has been overall confusion sur -
rounding the idea of wholism, some of which is understandable.
We are like children taking our first steps as we begin to explore
this new idea. As we will see, the advances in theoretical
physics and its investigation into matter and the true nature of the
universe open a new door into a more mature understanding of
wholism. In fact, as we take a penetrating look into the evolution
of scientific thought since the time of Einstein we will see that
"...the classical mechanistic worldview had to be abandoned at
the beginning of this century when quantum theory and relativity
theory – the two basic theories of modern physics – forced us to
adopt a much more subtle, wholistic and 'organic' view of
nature."[6] Seeing this, it becomes obvious that the traditional
health care establishment is based in a faulty, limited and
outdated premise – that of a mechanistic and fragmented theory
of reality.

Quantum theory and relativity arose from the investigation of
the microcosmic realm of atoms and subatomic particles – the
realm of very high energy states, of velocities approaching the
speed of light, of matter and antimatter, of complex quantum
field interactions, and of energy bundles (subatomic particles)
which can apparently move forward and backward in time! It is
important to realize, however, that this amazing description of
the atomic microcosmic world by the new physics (beginning
with Einstein's Special Theory of Relativity in 1905) did not
contradict the old physics (Newtonian physics). Rather it show -
ed that the old physics only applied to the three-dimensional
macrocosmic world involving relatively slow motion and low
energy states. But the perspective of scientific questioning
changed dramatically when Einstein showed in his famous
equation $E = mc^2$ that matter and energy were two forms of one
phenomenon, and further that time can be considered as a fourth
dimension of space. Einstein's concept of space-time implies

that all notions of absolute space or time "out there" are false. Broadly interpreted, it suggests that dimensional experience (i.e., that of space and time) is relative to the state of the observer.

As was pointed out earlier, virtually all areas of human endeavor in Western civilization have been rooted in the philo - sophical-scientific foundation of the old physics. We operate from a frame of reference in which we see ourselves as separate egos operating within an objective world "out there" some - where. The individual is divided into components of body, mind and feelings. This inner fragmentation is extended to the world "out there" and we further divide ourselves into different religions, political, ethnic and national groupings. Competition and exploitation characterize our approach to one another and our environment. In consequence, the fragmented body of humankind is riddled with misery and disease and totters on the edge of global self-destruction. Yet while we have been busy taking the mechanistic and fragmented view of reality to its ultimate conclusion, at the turn of the century the new physics began discovering a whole new direction. It has taken eight decades for the philosophical implication of this new direction to begin to break the surface of our collective consciousness and find application in everyday life. For the health care field and its emerging interest in wholism the discoveries of the new physics offer some profound implications:

"...relativity and quantum theory agree, in that they both imply the need to look on the world as an *undivided whole,* in which all parts of the universe, including the observer and his instruments, merge and unite in one totality... the new form of insight can perhaps best be called *Undivided Wholeness in Flowing Movement...* In this flow, mind and matter are not separate

35

substances. Rather they are different aspects of one whole and unbroken movement."[7]

"The philosophical implication of quantum mechanics is that all the things in our universe (including us) that appear to exist independently are actually part of one all-encompassing organic pattern, and that no parts of that pattern are ever really separate from it or from each other."[8]

"...the subatomic world appears as a web of relations between the various parts of a unified whole. Our classical notions, derived from our ordinary macroscopic experience, are not fully adequate to describe this world."[9]

Fritjof Capra, in *The Tao of Physics,* states the case that the wholistic, organic, interrelated, four-dimensional understanding of the universe and ourselves is not at all new. Eastern mystics and spiritual masters down through the centuries have described this knowledge in terms that are only now becoming intelligible to the Western mind. However, the mystics and masters have reached this knowing not by looking through electron micro - scopes or by elaborate experiments with particle accelerators, but through what they describe as direct experience of an expanded and transcendent state of being. Their approach was not from the "three-dimensional" perspective of physical and mental scientific investigation (the approach of the old physics), but from a "four-dimensional" vantage (like the new physics). From this vantage they describe an experience of being beyond space and time, a multidimensional experience of presence that "stands behind" the form of things. This presence is intelligent, creative and whole; it is our true nature, and its wisdom, if harmonized with, will direct all things perfectly from within. What is most remarkable – and examples of this abound in Capra's book – is that descriptions of the experience of this presence are remarkably similar to the Western physicist's description of reality via quantum and relativity theories. These descriptions are actually beyond the capability of present-day language – one reason why mystical portrayals of an expanded experience of being have seemed so esoteric to the Western mind. As Capra points out, "Our language and thought patterns have evolved in this three-dimensional world, therefore we find it extremely hard to deal with the four-dimensional reality of relativistic physics."[10]

The point here, however, is that the Eastern mystics and spiritual masters as well as present-day physicists, are trying to describe the same thing – a fundamental, organic principle or presence that pervades, animates and interrelates all forms, events and beings in the universe. This picture of reality, based in the revelations of the new physics, is beginning to shade the foundations of all areas of Western civilization, based as it has been on the old, fragmented, mechanistic model. As is always the case, when humanity is on the verge of a quantum leap in perspective, there is considerable opposition among the entrenched establishments based in the old-world view. We see this in the health care field – there is resistance, for example, to treating human beings as living, dynamic, multidimensional organisms – part of a fundamental underlying whole. But the movement toward this understanding is inexorable. As Larry Dossey, M.D., in *Space, Time and Medicine* points out, "Oneness and Unity are qualities of our universe. Our tendency to think of the world in terms of non-interacting parts violates the most accurate descriptions of the world we have, those of modern physics. These descriptions of the universe tell us that the 'parts' are illusions, understandable only in relation to all other parts. Subatomic particles are comprehended only through

37

their relationships with all other subatomic particles, and the same can be said for massive bodies – planets, stars, galaxies."[11] Dossey also points out that "We have nothing to lose by a reexamination of fundamental assumptions of our models of health; on the contrary, we face the extraordinary possibility of fashioning a system that emphasizes life instead of death, and unity and oneness instead of fragmentation, dark - ness, and isolation."[12] In fact, expanding on Dr. Dossey's thoughts, we could postulate that the forms of illness suffered by humankind today have their hidden origins in our flawed conception of reality. After all, if we see ourselves as isolated, unrelated fragments, fighting our way through a hostile, diseased, chaotic world, this view has to have its effects. We see these effects in the current epidemic proportions of fear, anxiety, depression, tension and loneliness – and we now know that stressful emotions contribute to most (if not all) forms of physical disease.

So we see a new understanding of ourselves and our world being born, and the experience of this is not confined to Eastern mystics, spiritual masters and theoretical physicists. It is a movement, rather, available to those who are compelled and willing to begin to experience things in a new way. This "way of stillness" at first may have little meaning to the Western mind; we equate stillness with nonaction, and action and achievement are everything in the West. But when understood and exper - ienced, the way of stillness is seen to be the doorway to *right* action within the vision of reality implied by the new physics.

We can't, however, think and theorize our way into the way of stillness. The way of stillness is a transcendent experience beyond the confines of our usual "three-dimensional aware - ness." Our language and thought patterns are so habitually three-dimensional that we find it impossible to think or even imagine in "higher-dimensional terms." As Capra points out, "We have no direct sensory experience of the four-dimensional space-time nor of the other relativistic concepts... We cannot experience the four-dimensional space-time world with our senses, but can only observe its three-dimensional 'images'."[13]

Experience, then, of "fourth-dimensional consciousness," is not a matter of simply shifting from three to four dimensions, like shifting your car from third to fourth gear. Rather, it implies a "quantum shift" in perspective, a shift that moves one into an experience of an underlying transcendent reality – transcendent in the sense that the "three-dimensional" physical, mental and emotional perceptive apparatus is not fully adequate to contain and grasp the experience.

While modern physicists have called the transcendent under - lying reality the quantum field, the fourth dimension and the implicate order, others have described this reality as Inner Nature, Divine Presence, Being, The Tao, Innate Intelligence, Life and Wholism. All the terms, whether from the physicist or non-physicist, point to the fact that there is an intelligent inner order within everything which unfolds itself from an invisible higher dimension into visible material form. Because Western science seeks to understand the nature of reality by an exam - ination into only visible material forms, the effort is doomed to confusion and failure. This approach is analogous to examining the reflection in the mirror instead of that which is being reflected. Ultimately, it has been an attempt by science to circumvent a conclusion that is unavoidable – that there is a creative, living, intelligent essence that pervades, animates and coordinates the material universe. This multidimensional living presence eludes our current forms of objective, scientific investigation – obviously so. It is interesting to note that the goal of science has always been to discover order and meaning: to discover the truth. But science excludes the existence of this living presence, and scientific investigation has been in keeping with the false premise that the material universe is an inanimate machine which has evolved out of chaos and is doomed to dissolve back into it. As a result we have torn our world apart seeking to find the rhyme and reason, but have only intensified our experience of alienation and loneliness in consequence. Finally, we begin to glimpse that the answer cannot be uncovered by tearing things apart.

The way of stillness is an approach that begins with the premise of wholeness, life and meaning. The experience of stillness is based in the understanding that there is no need to search for meaning in Life because Life is inherently meaning-ful. Knowledge and understanding are not gained through dissection, but rather through the experience of connection in the whole. There is intelligence and design within the whole, and each aspect of the whole has its own Inner Nature which unfolds from within. As with the acorn that contains the mighty oak within its essence, the right soil and climate are needed for the Inner Nature of things to unfold rightly into material form. When the external climate is in harmony with Inner Nature, there is no trying and struggling; the seed simply releases its inherent design and grows. This is the way of stillness – the external three-dimensional world receptive to and in harmony with Inner Nature. Here the oak tree has triumphed where humankind has failed.

Our external three-dimensional world of body, mind and heart has not been still – has not been posed, receptive and willing to be unfolded. Rather it has been the source of deafening noise, confusion and destruction. As human beings we have agreed with Descartes, seeing ourselves separate from our world and each other; individual egos with a body that can think and feel, but no more. Firmly believing that we are merely three-dimensional beings, we have been functioning like a car without the driver – clearly a dangerous game. In this analogy the car operates from the premise that it is capable of driving itself and arriving at a self-determined destination. But obviously the car is not capable of driving itself, or of making the quantum shift into becoming the driver; the driver is possessed of a whole other reality of existence – from the car's perspective, a transcendent reality. Just as the car can never, no matter how hard it tries, become the driver, neither can human beings, making a three-dimension approach, come to experience (even using modern technology) the transcendent dimension from which Inner Nature flows. It is only the way of stillness that makes possible this quantum shift in identity from the car to the driver: a stillness of body, mind and heart, which is not som - nambulance and unconsciousness, but a perceptive, receptive alertness. How does this happen? It would appear that if our earth and its inhabitants are to survive, and if we wish to discover the experience of true health and wholeness, we must find out.

**Notes:**
1 Fritjof Capra, *The Tao of Physics,* Shambhala Publications, Boston, 1975, p. 9.
2 ibid.
3 Fritjof Capra, *The Turning Point,* Simon & Schuster, New York, 1982, p. 60.
4 ibid. p. 146
5 ibid. p. 123 & 145.
6 Fritjof Capra, *The Tao of Physics,* p. 43.
7 David Bohm, *Wholeness and The Implicate Order,* Routledge & Kegan Paul, London, 1980, p.11.
8 Gary Zukav, *The Dancing Wu Li Masters,* William Morrow, New York, 1979, p. 48.
9 Fritjof Capra, *The Tao of Physics,* p. 144.

10 ibid. p. 136.
11 Larry Dossey, MD., *Space, Time and Medicine,*
    Shambhala Publications, Boston, 1982, p.115.
12 ibid. p. 142.
13 Fritjof Capra, *The Tao of Physics,* p. 156-157.

# From Person to Planet

## by Dawson Church

As we have unearthed the remains of ancient civilizations from China to the Americas, their surviving artifacts allow us to draw conclusions about their level of development. The types of implements they were able to forge informs us of their metal - lurgy and level of scientific achievement. The tools they fashion - ed allow us to conjecture as to their medical practices, crafts and manufacturing abilities. If they leave decipherable written records, we can glimpse their history, mythology, and trade agreements.

From these material artifacts we can reconstruct the material lives of the human beings involved with some degree of accur - acy. How big were their cities? How developed was their agri - culture? How far did their architecture spread? Less enduring, though, are their accomplishments of spirit. Were they happy? Were they rigid and immobile in their attitudes, or flexible and adaptable? What was the quality of their human interactions?

This material, physical-level approach leaves us with the habit of characterizing cultures as "stunted," "civilized," or "advanced"[1] on the basis of the quantity and complexity of the rubble they left behind them. From material data we can draw material conclusions. Yet how incomplete this picture of a par - ticular ancient civilization is; how dearly we would like to have an inkling of the intangible aspects of their lives. Our own

*Dawson Church is a successful businessman and writer residing in New York City. He is the author of many articles on holistic health, the emerging planetary culture, and Soviet-American relations, as well as organizing and speaking at conferences and exchanges on these themes. He is a long-time proponent of a vigorous, inspired, practical spirituality in the workplace, home and relationships. He is a graduate of Baylor University with a degree in communications.*

society has carried material achievement further than any civilization of which we are aware, yet, paradoxically, 'having it all' has taught us that the human spirit can starve even while surrounded by material prosperity. We have learned by our own example that material advantage alone is barren without an expansion and enrichment of man's inner life.

Set in the context of the evolution of our planet, how are we to characterize the ascent of man? Given that measuring the height to which different civilizations have been able to pile rocks one on top of the other is a very partial yardstick by which to measure the meaning of man upon planet Earth, what non-material scale may we employ to measure the degree of man's civilization? The great French scholar Teilhard de Chardin points out that, as we study the whole sweep of evolution, and es - pecially hominid evolution from pre-history to modern times, the index by which we may measure development is: conscious - ness. It becomes more complex and concentrated the higher a species sits on the evolutionary ladder.

"The natural history of living creatures amounts on the exterior to the gradual establishment of a vast nervous system," writes Teilhard, thus "it therefore corresponds on the interior to the installation of a psychic state coextensive with the earth. On the surface, we find the nerve fibres and ganglions; deep down, consciousness."[2]

Earliest man was characterized by small-scale social organization along the lines of the family, clan or tribe. With the invention of agriculture and the development of permanent settlements, a larger, fixed unit known as the village became common. As trade, transportation and communications became more elaborate, towns and cities grew up. As these became or - ganized into larger units, we find states developing, and it is at this level of nations that we find most human culture today.

Looking beyond the bric-a-brac produced by each level of development, an obvious feature emerges: the growth of the scale of the idea of community.

The first communities were small, roving tribal units. They faced an uncertain and often hostile world, which was a great deal larger than the clan and vastly more powerful. If we put ourselves into the mind of a Neolithic man, we find ourselves looking out at a world which is full of threats from outside: lightning, invasion and savage beasts. Other tribes threaten us. The weather is unpredictable and uncontrollable. The environ - ment abounds with animal predators stronger and fiercer than we. Our survival culture taboos loom far larger than our indiv - idual will and intent, for to contravene them means ostracism by the rest of our clan and almost certain death.

The circle of people we can trust is very small: the rest of our clan, with whom we are bonded by the very need to survive. We must accommodate any interpersonal conflict that arises, for to leave the tribe is impossible: a single human being cannot survive on his own.[3]

We now leap three thousand years ahead, to inhabit the mind of a Celtic villager. Our unit of communal consciousness is now the village. It is in the context of the survival of the village that we survive. In the village we will grow up, trade, marry and die. As we tend our crops we learn to co-operate with nature, making the physical world our ally. We build huts to protect us from the sun and rain. Our sense of *greater self* extends beyond our little family, to all the different families which inhabit the village, and band together when threatened. Outside our huts and fields, though, there is an unknown and unknow - ably vast world, into which few ever venture.

Fifty generations on, we live in a town, and we are proud of the accomplishments of our settlement. We trade with places many leagues hence, and we are excited by the news and ideas that come from them. Our town has grown so large that there are actually people who live in it who we do not know, whose faces we may never have seen! But we would proudly man the walls with them were an invader to threaten. There are no wild beasts inside the town walls, but plenty of human enemies without.

Two thousand years later, trade and communication between towns has made people so alike that we can now think of ourselves as a nation. Men of towns, cities and villages all sub - scribe to a larger identity, the identity of our *country*. Our sense of identity extends all the way to our national borders, and though these are just invisible lines drawn on the ground by an imaginary hand, we will fight for them, uniting with our countrymen from town and village, millions and millions strong. We have diplomatic relations with other countries, and while we cannot always understand their ways, we know we can at least talk to someone of our own country.

# Growth of Humanity
# As the Growth of Community

As we review the development of man from the earliest times to the present, we see him conceiving of "community" in larger and larger units, from the individual to the band, from the band to the village, from the village to the town, from the town to the race, and finally the nation-state.

Linked to the physical and material development of our civilizations, our sense of identity has grown. The earliest hunter-gatherer had a tiny compartment for "me" and an un - thinkably huge compartment for "other than me" which had to accommodate the whole world. By contrast, today we can con - ceive of a national "we" which includes millions of individuals whose faces are unknown to us. The growth of civilization, then, can be measured by the growth of the size of the sense of identity *beyond* the individual human being. The quantum of consciousness has grown from the most rudimentary social groupings of man to the integrated planetary psychosphere of today.

At this point in its development the human race finds itself in the midst of the next great leap of consciousness: the leap to planetary identity. We feel the horror of a war ten-thousand miles away, played out on our television screen. We are affected by the picture of a hungry child halfway around the world, and we respond. The planetary communications complex we have created connects events separate in space and even time. It functions, like the ganglia of the human nervous system, as the neural pathways of the global brain. These communications mechanisms have awakened us to the extant fact of a global identity, through both the messages they transmit and by their very existence. Our new paradigm of community is inter - national, inter-racial, super-individual. It compels us to admit our own unhealthiness by virtue of our connection with this diseased human race; we can no longer say, "*We* are healthy, but *they* are unhealthy."

We can also, in this context, no more envision the destruc - tion of our enemies without destroying ourselves. To do so would be as absurd as the stomach seeking to destroy the hand in the interests of its own "security." We have even built dooms - day weapons in order to teach ourselves that we cannot destroy another without destroying all.[4] There is, in fact, no "other," only ourselves. "Nuclear weapons are a symbol: we can no longer eliminate that which is not like us without eliminating ourselves. 'In the nuclear age,' as one Soviet Central Committee advisor wrote, 'the logic is new: old notions of strength turn out to be weakness, victory becomes loss, attack – suicide...we have our Soviet logic, Americans have their logic, and the

Europeans have theirs. But in the nuclear age we must have a single logic or none at all.'"5

This clearly underlines that the quantum of survival now is not the nation, and the enemies are not outside of ourselves. Bill Ury, of the Harvard Nuclear Negotiation Project, commented that "The nuclear problem is one of consciousness, not of weapons systems. The British have nuclear weapons, but we aren't worried about them, because the consciousness is differ - ent." The threats that humanity faces today are not external storms; they come from within, and are simply the patterns of the past. If we refuse to renovate our consciousness, acting as if the old paradigm is true: "My nation will destroy your nation in the interests of my security," our minds will carry the seeds of destruction from the past into the present. It is this "creed outworn" (Wordsworth) from which we must liberate our - selves, growing into the conceptual patterns appropriate to planetary citizens.

The last quarter of the twentieth century sees the human species facing what Buckminster Fuller called our "final exam - ination," to determine whether we can grow in consciousness to a vision of the world in which everything is me: "We Are The World." If we fail, we will destroy ourselves. If we destroy ourselves, we will have failed. We do not have the option, like Noah, of building an ark "to the saving of *his* house" alone.6 The Ark of the twentieth century is the planet Earth, and to save life, the the five billion neurons of her helmsman must make the leap to the "planetization of consciousness."7 The outlines of this idea have been emerging through scientists and mystics for many years. In 1932, J.B.S. Haldane wrote:

"We do not find obvious evidences of life or mind in so-called inert matter, and we naturally study them most easily where they are most completely manifested, but if the scientific point of view is correct, we shall ultimately find them, at least in rudimentary forms, all through the universe.

Now if the co-operation of some thousands of millions of cells in our brain can produce our conscious - ness, the idea becomes vastly more plausible that the co-operation of humanity...may determine what Comte calls a Great Being."[8]

Our most advanced visionaries are already describing the next step: the "Great Being" of our collective planet assuming her place within the community of the stars.[9] In this view, humans are the "global brain"[10] of earth, or Gaia,[11] who is herself an earth-sized cell of the cosmic body. This vision of selfhood embraces the entire universe, and so far transcends individual human boundaries as to qualify as a whole different order of identity: transcendent identity in the whole. As Albert Einstein expressed it:

"A human being is part of the whole, called by us 'Universe,' a part limited in time and space. He exper - iences himself, his thoughts and feelings as something separated from the rest – a kind of optical delusion of his consciousness. This delusion is a kind of prison for us, restricting us to our personal desires and to affection for a few persons nearest to us.

Our task must be to free ourselves from this prison by widening our circle of compassion to embrace all living creatures and the whole of nature in its beauty."[12]

The discoveries of holistic healing have taught us that the size of the area of our consideration must expand if treatment is to be effective. If we are treating spots on the liver, no sensible physician treats the spot as though it were isolated from the liver. Likewise, no wise physician treats the liver as though it were a fragment isolated from the body. And no complete physician treats a body as though it were divorced from soul and spirit. And in the long view, treating the individual as though personal health were paramount, or even possible outside of the sustaining planetary "Earth Mother," ignores the crisis/opportun - ity point at which we as a species find ourselves. Looking at just the material aspects of disease leads us to the same incomplete conclusions as studying just the material evidences of a civilization.

## Wellness: Why Bother?

Why do we wish to be healthy, and what is the relationship between disease and fragmentary thinking?

From the standpoint of the whole Earth, the irrational passions by which human beings may be ruled are hideously destructive: fear, greed, envy, hatred, and so on. From the glo - bal perspective, it may be very valuable that such an individual be unhealthy. This limits his scope of working mischief! If he were well, his ability to project these destructive emotions into disruptive action would be enhanced. Illness may thus be something of a planetary defense mechanism, a reaction against the baneful inner states which human beings have nurtured within themselves.

Smaller countries are in the habit, likewise, of taking the superpowers to task[13] for their lack of accommodation of each other and their antagonistic stance which inevitably embroils smaller nations. Yet when one examines their relations with their their neighbors, the "non-aligned" states are no more saintly than the nuclear club. If these smaller "planetary organs" were able to project their phobias further, they would undoubtedly be perceived as behaving as badly as their bulky cousins. It is easy to name half a dozen "sick man" countries whose weakness undoubtedly contributes to the overall welfare of the whole.

It is therefore most appropriate to ask: "Why should we be healed?" If our being personally well will result in a net increase in the amount of ill action in the world, then from the point of view of the whole, our illness is a blessing! The situation is analogous to that of a bully, who is temperamentally inclined to terrorize other children. If he grows up to be a sickly, 4'6", 85 lb. man, he can do less damage on the physical level than if he were a hulking giant. Human illness, then, taken as a whole, may thus be one of Gaia's self-correcting or "homeostatic" mechanisms. The word "homeostasis" derives from a principle enumerated by the nineteenth-century French physiologist Claude Bernard, who maintained that "all the vital mechanisms, varied as they are, have only one object: that of preserving constant the conditions of life."[14] In *The Global Brain,* Peter Russell writes:

"An example of homeostasis is the human body's maintenance of a temperature of about 98.6 degrees Fahrenheit, the ideal temperature for the majority of the body's metabolic processes. Although the external temperature may vary by scores of degrees, our internal temperature seldom varies by more than a degree or two...Such processes are found not only in the human body and in all living systems but also within Gaia herself.

Gaia appears to maintain planetary homeostasis in a variety of ways, monitoring and modifying many key components in the atmosphere, oceans, and soil."[15]

If indeed illness is a planetary homeostatic device, the opposite may be true: that as human beings develop the attitudes appropriate to planetary nurture, making common cause with the forces that are moving us toward integration, balance, abun - dance, and the other characteristics of life, they may, almost as a side effect, win physical health. And as, individually, we leap in consciousness from a self-centered world view to a whole world view we may be doing more than we could ever guess for the welfare of the earth. As Lord Exeter has expressed it:

> "We see the evidences of integration on every hand all around us, reaching into the uttermost ends of the uni - verse. Only...the state of self-centeredness in man" – the old paradigm – "establishes the inevitability of disinte - gration."
> "All the various fields of the...healing arts are designed to help keep us together, as though it would be disastrous if this supposedly civilized world fell apart. But the world of human construction is based in the consciousness of self-centeredness and this false foun - dation results inevitably in disintegration."[16]

Ceasing to make personal healing the defining icon of the healing professions, we instead begin to link healer and patient in the urgent quest for planetary wellness. It isn't just that freedom from disease would be nice. The penalties for us as human beings are extreme, should we collectively "fail" our survival test. A patient in perfect health is a meaningless accomplishment if the planet is destroyed. A recent bumper sticker said "A single nuclear warhead could ruin your whole day!" We have reached the opposite end of the spectrum from the caveman: our individual survival is now dependent upon maintaining the integrity of the whole.

It is extremely interesting to look at cancer in the light of these recent understandings of how Gaia may function. Some authorities see a link between "the way a malignant growth develops in the human being, eventually destroying the body on which it is ultimately dependent, and the way in which humanity appears to be eating its way indiscriminately across the surface of the planet, disrupting and possibly destroying its planetary host."[17] If Gaia is indeed a living organism, then it is obviously in her best interest to rid herself of those cells which, like the rogue cancer cells in a human body, disrupt the function of the whole. "Cancer is not a villain separate from me. Rather, it is a result of each of us, and humankind as a whole, operating out of control. If we view each human being as a cell in the collective body of humanity, individual cancer cells are apparent, as well as collective tumors."[18] In a general sense then, human illness may thus be seen as Gaia's homoestatic mechanism for sup - pressing the effectiveness of humanity's destructive power.

By the same token, co-operation with the whole, and the patterns and characteristics of the whole, is both life-supporting and life-giving to the individual who practices these values: life-supporting in that it contributes to the overall wellness of the whole, and life-giving in that it affirms the place in the whole of that individual, who is nurtured as one of "Nature's own."

## The Planetary Role of the Healer

What is the practical relevance of this "leap to planetization" for the healer and the patient?

Beyond treating the symptom, the physician has the responsibility of representing wellness to the patient, of being a totem of wellness rather than a figure associated only with disease. Problems, disruptions, disturbances and the like – what

Jung termed the "troubling presence of the shadow" – come to everyone, including both doctor and patient. But it is the way we handle them that illumines our inner attitudes. We may use these seeming adversities to emphasize wellness: "What's right with you is the point. What's wrong with you is beside the point."

The qualities of our invisible attitudes and visible actions may strengthen or weaken the "wellness field." The noted English scientist Rupert Sheldrake was the first to posit the existence of what he calls "morphogenic fields." He points to many examples of similar behavior in a wide variety of species, across time and space, in ways that are clearly not genetic or learned. He ascribes these phenomena to "fields" produced by like actions. These fields are reinforced every time a similar behavior takes place. These then tend to produce the same behavior in other members of the same species. In this view, the collective medical paradigm of the human race is an extension of the beliefs and practices of all those who practice medicine.

As individual practitioners change their attitudes and methods, insignificant though these may seem to be when considered as separate acts, they have a powerful combined effect on the concepts of wellness residing in the mass consciousness. Teilhard de Chardin maintains:

> "We are faced with a harmonized collectivity of con - sciousness equivalent to a sort of superconsciousness. The idea is that of the earth not only becoming covered by myriads of grains of thought, but becoming enclosed in a single thinking envelope so as to form, functionally, no more than a single vast grain of thought on the sidereal scale, the plurality of individual reflections grouping themselves together and reinforcing one another in the act of a single unanimous reflection."[19]

In this "super-consciousness," no thought by any healer at any time is outside the flow, or irrelevant. Every reflection feeds into the human paradigm of healing. The way we think is therefore intrinsically healing of the body of mankind – or it isn't. The choice is ours, and we are making it in everything we think, speak or act. "When asked if there would be a nuclear war, Carl Jung replied that he thought it depended on the number of *individuals* who could resolve the tension of opposites within themselves."[20]

The Hippocratic oath might be amended to say:

"You do solemnly swear, each man by whatever he holds most sacred, that you will be loyal to the whole - ness of life, and just and generous to all life forms; that you will lead your lives, practice your art, and keep your heart in uprightness and honor; that into whatsoever house you shall enter, it shall be for the bringing of wellness to the utmost of your power, you holding yourself far aloof from wrong, from corruption, from the temptation of disease-centered thinking; that you will exercise your art solely for the healing of your patients and will give no drug, perform no operation, and hold no attitude except for humility and reverence for the whole of life; that whatever you shall see or hear of the lives of men which is not fitting to be spoken, you will have no part in. Let each man bow his head in sign of acquiescence. If you be true to this your oath, you may be a true minister of healing to both person and planet; if you are forsworn, you will bring destruction upon all."

Perhaps in a distant day, when historians of the future look back on planet earth, they will have long since ceased to examine the height of the cities we build and the complexity of the artifacts we produce. Instead they will examine the stature of our ideas, the nobility of our attitudes, and the healing vibrance of the planetary psychosphere which is ours to co-create. If they do, they may say that, indeed, there were great healers at work in this age.

**Notes:**
1 Albert Tucker, *A History of English Civilization,*
Harper & Row, New York, 1972, pp. 6-15,
2 Teilhard de Chardin, *The Phenomenon of Man,*
Harper & Row, New York, 1975, p. 146.
3 Jean Auel, *The Clan of the Cave Bear,* Crown, 1980.
4 Carlson & Comstock, *Securing Our Planet,* Jeremy Tarcher,
Los Angeles, 1986, p. 287.
5 David Thatcher, *Earthrise: A Personal Responsibility,*
Foundation House, Loveland, 1987, p. 42.
6 Hebrews 11:7, King James Version.
7 *The Phenomenon of Man,* p. 252.
8 J.B.S. Haldane, Essay on Science and Ethics in
*The Inequality of Man,* Chatto, London, 1932, p. 113.
9 Ken Carey, *The Starseed Transmissions,* Uni-Sun Press,
Kansas City, 1982.
10 Peter Russell, *The Global Brain,* Jeremy Tarcher,
Los Angeles, 1983.
11 J.P. Lovelock, *Gaia: A New Look At Life on Earth,*
Oxford University Press, London, 1979.
12 Albert Einstein, quoted in *The Global Brain,* p. 145.
13 The Delhi Declaration, quoted in *Securing Our Planet,*
Carlson & Comstock, p. 281.
14 *The Global Brain,* p. 23.
15 ibid.
16 Lord Exeter, *On Eagle's Wings,* Two Continents/Mitre Press,
New York, 1977, p. 81.
17 *The Global Brain,* pp. 156-157.
18 *Earthrise: A Personal Responsibility,* p. 37.
19 *The Phenomenon of Man,* p. 252.
20 *Earthrise,* p. 42

# The Wounded Healer

## by Larry Dossey

Although life is an affair of light and shadows, we never accept it as such. We are always reaching towards the light and the high peaks. From childhood...we are given values which correspond only to an ideal world. The shadowy side of real life is ignored. Thus [we] are unable to deal with the mixture of light and shadow of which life really consists; [we] have no way of linking the facts of existence to [our] preconceived notions of absolutes. The links connecting life with universal symbols are therefore broken, and disintegration sets in.

— Miguel Serrano
*C.G. Jung and Hermann Hesse: A Record of Two Friendships*

"In the treatment process, something happens to the clinician as well as to the patient (e.g., fear, distancing, anger, frustration, joy, satisfaction, etc.). Frequently, [there occur] defensive maneuvers on the part of the clin - ician to avoid confronting the emotions and memories which the patient evokes... in the clinician. In shutting out a part of the patient, we also close off access to an

*Dr. Larry Dossey is a graduate of the Southwestern Medical School (M.D. 1967) in Dallas, TX. Following his internship, he served as a battalion surgeon in Vietnam. He is now a full-time practitioner of internal medicine and an organizer of the Dallas Diagnostic Association. He is also Chief of Staff at Medical City Dallas Hospital. He travels widely as a public speaker, in addition to his full-time practice. He lives in Dallas with his wife, Barbara, who is a critical care nurse, cardiovascular and biofeedback nurse specialist, and author of several books. As well as numerous articles, Dr. Dossey is the author of* Space, Time and Medicine *and* Beyond Illness. *(see p 240)*

This chapter is taken from *Beyond Illness* by Larry Dossey, © 1984. Reprinted by arrangement with Shambhala Publications, Inc., 300 Massachusetts Ave., Boston, MA 02115.

important part of ourselves. We can grow emotionally (if painfully) with our patients...if we can see beyond surgical 'repair,' patient 'compliance,' or drug 'efficacy.' Not that these latter are unimportant; but what whole are they a part of? What happens to us is as important as what happens to our patients. Indeed, what we allow ourselves to experience, both in ourselves and in our patients, decisively determines our diagnostic procedure, assessment of etiology, determination of prognosis, and formulation and implementation of a treatment plan. The philosophical and psychological question is not whether we will use ourselves in the clinical encounter, but how. This is axiomatic in all medicine."

–Howard F. Stein

"To say 'Thou' to a patient, and mean it, one must be able to utter 'I' to oneself. One can then stand *with* his patient, because he can stand alone with himself. This is the essence of medicine, of therapeutic communication, of life."

–Howard F. Stein

"...Eliade says '...the myth reveals the *deepest aspects* of reality.' That is, the language and imagery of mythology might be much closer to the nature of reality than are linear logic and abstract thinking, for if the real world is indeed holographic, then only the multivalent nature of the mythic image would be capable of sus - taining this vision and eliciting this understanding. The holographic-mythic image, wherein the whole is the part and the part is the whole, would be able to grasp [these] states of affairs... Mythological awareness is holo - graphic because it begins to transcend conventional boundaries — boundaries of space and time, and opposites and selves — and for that very reason alone, mythological awareness might be one step closer to the real world, 'the seamless coat of the universe,' as Whitehead put it."

— Ken Wilber

One of the greatest obstacles in understanding how health and illness form a unitary fact of our existence, how illness is as necessary as health in our lives, is our tendency to ignore life's darker side. In matters of health we focus only on the light and the high peaks, cringing from pain, suffering, and illness. We ignore these ignoble aspects of existence until we confront them in stark and undeniable ways and can no longer run from them. They may surface as illness in our own particular life, or in the death of a friend. But following the anguish we continue to attempt the impossible, to banish them from existence, looking only to the light. Yet it is a futile task. Deep within us we know we have created a lie and that sooner or later the next confrontation with the shadowy side of life must inevitably occur.

I am not proposing that we renounce optimism about our own health and revert to a morbid disposition wherein we continually dwell on our inevitable decline and demise, for this extreme is as one-sided as its opposite. I am not suggesting that physicians cease to hold out hope to those who are ill, assuring them instead that they must inevitably die — if not this time, then perhaps the next. I am proposing instead that we simply cannot have it the way we want it, for the simple and plain fact that light is not to be found without shadows, nor health without illness.

To suppose otherwise is to live a fantasy, a make-believe world. And to fail to acknowledge the dark side of health actually diminishes the healthiness we do feel – for it takes energy to live out falsity; it is draining to attempt to keep the lid on the pot of grimness. We pay a penalty for supposing that there is only the light, and the penalty is that the intensity of the light, our healthiness, is diminished.

## The Myth of the All-Powerful Physician

One of the most curious traditions that has persisted in modern medicine is the tradition of the all-powerful physician. This belief is pathological because it is a distortion to the grossest degree. It is a belief that endures because it fills a need – the need of the patient to deify his healer and to imbue him with superhuman abilities, and the need of certain physicians whose egos need the fantasy to continue. As long as the patient has a god-like figure looking after his welfare, things are safe. Any self-responsibility he might need to invoke on his own behalf to be healthy is minimized, for with an all-powerful physician at hand he is secure. After all, gods can "fix" anything. No matter the degree to which my health might fail, my physician-as-god can set it straight. And it is not surprising that many physicians do little to disavow this saintly mantle with which they are invested, allowing the show to go on rather than acknowledge their own limitations and ignorance.

This mutual participation by both doctors and patients in the myth of the all-powerful physician is one way in which we hide from the shadows. We need not acknowledge the dark side of illness and suffering as long as we have a god-healer at our disposal. True, illness will one day occur; but the mythological, god-like healers will summarily sweep it aside when it does supervene as if it were little more than a nuisance and a bother. With gods as our healers there is nothing but the light. The valleys and the shadows can be ignored.

The greatest healers, however, do not participate in this myth. They sense their own limitations as surely as they know their strengths. They know, too, the necessity of illness in human life and its dynamic interrelatedness with health. For them the light and shadows are both essential ingredients of healthiness, and they do not attempt to ignore one in favor of the other.

## The Myth of Chiron

Nowhere is the intrinsic fusion of health and illness more vividly illustrated than in the Greek mythological figure Chiron, whom the brilliant contemporary mythologist Carl Kerényi calls the wounded healer. Chiron was a centaur, half man and half horse. According to myth, the hero Heracles was received by the centaur Pholos at his cave. He was presented with a jar of rich wine, the scent of which attracted the other centaurs. Unaccustomed to the wine, the centaurs began to fight; and in the battle which followed, one of the arrows shot by Heracles wounded Chiron in the knee. Following the instructions of Chiron, Heracles tended to the wound, but because the arrow's tip bore the poison of the hydra the wound was incurable. Chiron thus could not be cured nor could he die, since he was immortal. He is an enigmatic figure: immortal but wounded, carrying within himself the godlike and the mortal at the same time.

From Mount Pelion, the site of his cave, he received and taught heroes their craft. Among them was Asclepius, who learned from Chiron the knowledge of herbs and power of the snake. Yet Chiron, the greatest teacher of medicine, ironically, could not heal himself. This was part of the wisdom which Chiron passed to Asclepius, the wisdom embodied in the wounding of the great healer.

## Physician and Teacher: An Intimate Relationship

The etymological meaning of the word "physician" is "teacher," an association symbolized powerfully in the relation - ship between Chiron and Asclepius. Robert J. Sardello, the psychologist and writer, has drawn attention to the similar role of the teacher and healer. In his penetrating treatise, "Teaching as Myth," his observations about teaching have the strongest relevance to the role of the physician:

> "Our teaching often does not resemble that of this great - est of mythical teachers, Chiron. As long as a teacher stands totally in the light, stands as one who knows, facing those who do not know, the teacher remains un - aware of his own woundedness and does not participate in the learning enterprise. An original and originating image of teaching is split radically into two parts as long as the teacher imagines himself as one who knows and the student as one in need of instruction. The student must stand in total darkness if the teacher stands totally in the light. Such a split image identifying teaching with knowledge and learning with ignorance can be main - tained only through power. This attitude is like that of the physician who believes that he does the curing rather than being the occasion through which curing comes as a gift. And like such a physician, such power is main -

tained by authority, by speaking in jargon, presenting oneself as a specialist and seeking professional status."[1]

This is a grotesque view of teaching, a dehumanizing, in - humane scenario which places one human in domination over another who becomes the inferior supplicant. It is the role all too often enacted in the doctor-patient relationship. The physician forgets his own woundedness, his own imminent or potential sickness, his own inexorable death. He is willing to be elevated by the patient to the role of the god-like. The error occurs on both the parts of the physician, renouncing his own fallibility and woundedness in favor of deification, and the patient, who creates a god and claims him for his own private healer.

It is frequently supposed that this type of relationship is actually desirable, for from his position of ultimate respect and admiration the physician can motivate the patient to make certain changes, to follow advice, to have surgery, to take medications, etc. Nothing is lost if the all-powerful, glorified, and deified physician uses his power benevolently. If the patient's best interests are kept in the foreground, this type of relationship can be tremendously therapeutic, it is alleged. It does no good in this scenario to remind the physician of his own woundedness, for it is power that counts in this relationship, not weakness. Why, if the patient actually felt his physician to be 'wounded' he would lose respect. After all, who wants his physician to be comprom - ised in some way? It is best to let the concept of the wounded healer remain in mythical lore.

I believe that this kind of relationship, in spite of the fact that it is frequently preferred by both doctors and patients, is sadly off base. It perpetuates the idea that woundedness is abhorrent; we especially must not speak of it in healers; it is only power and health that count. The interconnectedness of health and illness in human lives goes unnoticed. It might be argued that we should not object to this sort of doctor-patient relationship if it were highly effective. But here is the point on which it most miserably fails: it simply does not work therapeutically as it ought. We must now see why.

## The Doctor-Patient Relationship:
## A Living Archetype

The Jungian psychiatrist Adolf Guggenbühl-Craig has described the doctor-patient relationship in a provocative way. In his book, *Power in the Helping Professions,* he states:

> "The 'healer-patient' relationship is as fundamental as is that of man-woman, father-son, mother-child. It is archetypal, in the sense expounded by C.G. Jung; i.e., it is an inherent, potential form of human behavior. In archetypal situations the individual perceives and acts in accordance with a basic schema inherent in himself, but which in principle is the same for all men."[2]

The doctor-patient relationship, then, is contained within nature. It is primordial, something inborn, an innate behavior seeking expression in the appropriate circumstance. It is called forth when we are sick, injured, or about to die. At those times we look to healers as naturally as a mother looks to her child. At such times we are duplicating behavior of countless members of our species who have looked to their own healers, persons who have had names other than "doctor": shaman, curandero, witch doctor. To look to the healer during times of affliction is as natural as seeking food or water.

On the surface, archetypal behavior seems simpler than it is. It seems as if, for example, the mother is simply reacting to her child, an object "out there." A woman responds to a man, who is himself an object apart from her. Patients respond to healers who, too, are objects possessing some fundamental status of their own distinct from that of the patient. But the basic situation is more complex. Every archetypal situation contains a polarity – that is, both poles are contained within the same individual. To reiterate, as Guggenbühl-Craig says, "Each of us is born with poles of the archetype within us." And, "... in human psych - ology as we know it, both poles are contained within the same individual."[3]

This is a crucial point because it flies in the face of our ordinary concept of the doctor-patient relationship. We suppose that on the one hand there is the healer, and that on the other stands the patient, who is little more than a passive object to whom and for whom certain things are done. But the concept of archetype tells us that this way of thinking is misconstrued. It suggests that a polarity exists within both individuals that constitute the archetype, the healer and the patient. It suggests in no uncertain terms that the patient contains something of the healer within his being, and that the healer is simultaneously the patient as well – containing, as it were, his own woundedness.

Guggenbühl-Craig clarifies how the polarity of the archetype operates:

"A child awakens maternal behavior in its mother. In the psyche of every woman there is the inborn potentiality of motherly behavior within the mother-child situation, which in some mysterious way must mean that the child is already contained within the mother, somewhat in Goethe's sense when he wrote: 'Did our eye not contain sun's power, how could it perceive the sun at all?' Perhaps we should not speak of a mother archetype, a child archetype or a father archetype. It might be better to talk of a mother-child or a father-child archetype."[4]

Extending these analogies to the doctor-patient relationship, there is, then, something of each in both: the polarity of the healer and the one-to-be-healed are contained within the healer and the patient, and there is, in fact, only a single archetype which embraces both doctor and patient, not a different archetype for each.

Why bother to struggle with formulations such as these? What difference does it make what ancient mythology has contended about 'wounded healers,' or what Jungian psychological theory asserts about arcane constructions such as archetypes and polarities? It is my belief that there are few things more important in modern medicine than that we get these issues straight -- far more important than, for example, setting up a Manhattan-type Project to search for 'the cure' for cancer, heart disease, or any malady whatever. Unless we understand such basic notions as how we ourselves, patients and physicians, are constituted at heart, all subsequent attempts at healing will, in some sense, fall short, and all apparent cures will be nothing more than counterfeit. We will continue to flail about in medical research and in clinical medicine in our endless attempts to banish the shadows and retain only the light, or attempt to fill in all the valleys in our lives while retaining the peaks. It will not matter greatly whether we actually do find 'the cure' for whatever affliction, for, without a sure knowledge of how we are constellated, we will never know even who it is that has been cured, nor who it was that did the curing.

Yet what does it mean to say that both poles of the archetype exist within the physician and the patient? The statement need not be defended simply through metaphor or psychological theory. It can be taken literally, and it can be described in strictly

70

scientific terms. Let us consider that the sick person contains his own healer. What is the proof?

## The Inner Healer: More Than Myth

Examples could be endlessly produced, one of which is the careful study of Jerome Frank, at Johns Hopkins Medical School.[5] Frank studied the speed of healing of surgical wounds in the immediate post-operative period. He found that those patients healed fastest who had faith, trust and confidence in the surgeon and the nursing staff. On the other hand, slower wound healing occurred in those patients who did not trust their physicians, and who were reluctant and afraid. This type of study goes beyond the metaphorical use of the term inner healer, and relates the concept to something as concrete as the healing of actual surgical wounds. The end point is measurable: The inner healer is something inward, whose effects are quantifiable. As such, it is not just a topic that must be dealt with by mystics and philosophers, but it is a fit concern for bioscientists as well. It is important to point out, for we must constantly remind ourselves that we are not just speaking psychologically or poetically, but physiologically as well.

The polar expression, then, of the wounded healer who is mythically represented by Chiron, the centaur-teacher of Asclepius, is that of 'the healthy wounded.' The healthy wound - ed are all of us, for we all have within us the inner healing potential demonstrated in Frank's study. It is not for us to create, for it is there, existing inwardly as a force for healing as surely as there exists within us the capacity to fall ill. This is the polarity of the archetype which all men contain.

It is becoming recognized, through the best of medical research, that patients do have self-corrective, innate, inward, self-healing capacities. In a variety of disease states these so-called 'factors of consciousness' – emotions, attitudes, feeling states of various sorts – have emerged as potent factors in healing.[6]

## The Inner Patient

But the sword of the archetype polarity cuts both ways:

"It is not very difficult to imagine the healing factor in the patient. But what about the physician? Here we encount - er the archetype of the 'wounded healer.' Chiron, the centaur who taught Asclepius the healing arts, himself suffered from incurable wounds. In Babylon there was a dog-goddess with two names: as Gula she was death and as Labartu, healing. In India Kali is the goddess of the pox and at the same time its curer. The mythological image of the wounded healer is very widespread. Psychologically this means not only that the patient has a physician within himself, but also there is a patient in the doctor."[7]

It is this concept that is much harder for healers to swallow, for it is an admission of an integral, inescapable weakness. The recognition of fallibility comes hard for many modern healers. And, not surprisingly, we physicians expend ingenious efforts to conceal this eternal fact. This dilemma, however, has been faced by healers of all times, not just our own, and is expressed by Guggenbühl-Craig:

"It is not easy for human psyche to bear the tension of polarities. The ego loves clarity and tries to eradicate inner ambivalence. This need for the unequivocal can bring about a certain splitting of polar archetypes. One pole may be repressed and continue operating in the un - conscious, possibly causing psychic disturbances. The repressed part of the archetype can be projected onto the outer world."[8]

One of the most difficult admissions for many modern physicians, who have been schooled in an era when the medical credo is to do, to act, and to cure, is that of woundedness. It becomes more expedient to do something, sometimes anything, for which the doctor is frequently praised ("He was willing to take her case when no other doctor would; he was willing to operate in spite of overwhelming odds; no matter that Mother died, the doctor tried!"). It has become extraordinarily difficult in modern clinical medicine to do nothing. Doing nothing is taken too frequently as an expression of impotence, of fallibility. It is a reminder to the physician of something he'd rather forget: the fact of his own woundedness.

There are many physicians to whom the fact of their own woundedness is apparent, and they handle this knowledge with a grace that empowers them as healers. Yet others do not. And the unfortunate way that the inner fact of woundedness is too often dealt with is through projecting it onto the external world in an attempt to rid oneself of something painful. Far better that someone else should be wounded, weak, or fallible than I, so the rationalization goes. And the object of the physician's projected weakness is all too often the patient, as the following incident illustrates.

## The Story of Tom B.

Tom B. was taken to the coronary care unit of a major hospital after collapsing with chest pain and shortness of breath at home. He was seventy-eight years old, had already sustained two heart attacks, and suffered from high blood pressure. Although he took his prescription medications religiously, he had been unable to stop smoking and lose weight, a fact which always irritated his doctor who never failed to remind Tom about it.

Tom's wife had called an ambulance immediately and then called Dr. Ponder, who said he would meet his patient in the emergency room. Upon arrival of both patient and physician at the hospital's emergency room, resuscitation efforts were continued, having been initiated by the paramedics who found Tom without any detectable blood pressure and with an erratic, ineffective heart rhythm. Finally, with intravenous tubing streaming from both arms, Tom was moved to the coronary care unit of the hospital with the diagnosis of acute myocardial infarction and congestive heart failure.

Tom's elderly wife remained in the background all the while; she didn't want to interfere. After all, Dr. Ponder had rescued Tom on two previous occasions following heart attacks, and she had to believe he would do so again. Even though she was burning with a desire to hear from the doctor about how her husband was doing, she remained unobtrusive, getting second-hand bits of information from the nurses who were scurrying in and out of the room. She thought it odd, though, that Dr. Ponder had no time for her. After all, he had to know she was there, for it was she who had placed the call, telling him she was en route to the hospital with her husband.

An hour later, following her husband's transfer to the coronary care unit, she stood weeping outside the swinging doors that guarded its entry. Still no word. Then without warning both doors burst open and Dr. Ponder emerged, obviously very angry. My God, she thought, why is he angry? Any emotion, she allowed herself to think, would be more appropriate than anger.

Fuming, Dr. Ponder exploded, "Your husband is making this very difficult! He refuses to cooperate with anything I do!"

Dr. Ponder stood there, glowering at her, his face flushed and diaphoretic, gripping a stethoscope in one hand. Mrs. B. sensed he was waiting for some response from her. She knew she had to say something, anything, and through her tears she stammered, "Oh Dr. Ponder, please forgive Tom, I know he doesn't mean it!"

Dr. Ponder did not acknowledge the apology, but wheeled abruptly, disappearing through the double doors, still streaming anger behind him. Mrs. B. never saw her husband alive again. Within an hour he was dead.

I fortunately do not believe most physicians behave in crucial situations like Dr. Ponder; this incident is related only as a classic example of how healers repress part of their own archetype (their woundedness, their weakness, their fallibility, their helplessness) and project it onto the external world where it frequently becomes the patient's weakness, not the doctor's ("He refuses to cooperate with anything I do!"). But the healer may project his own wounds in a more subtle way than did Dr. Ponder. For instance, it may not be the poor patient himself onto whom the physician projects his weakness, but the disease itself ("This is the worst case of high blood pressure I have ever seen in my career as a physician!"). In this case the patient does not answer for the doctor's weaknesses, but some impersonal entity called disease. This disease-as-enemy approach is very com - mon. The doctor-patient relationship can constellate strongly around this common foe without either having to admit to the shadows within themselves.

Another variation on the theme of how the healer avoids the recognition and admission of his own woundedness is by projecting the failure onto 'the system' — "We just don't have a cure for this problem yet." Here the scapegoat becomes the entire medical edifice itself, which has so far failed to produce a suitable remedy. It is not the physician who is weak. He is simply making-do the best he can, working with the tools at hand.

## The Harm in Denying the Inner Polarity

I am not suggesting that there is not some justification to the occasional use of statements such as these. It is when patient and doctor actually begin to believe that these represent reality that great harm occurs. For when each denies the inner polarity of his own archetype, certain events predictably follow: for the physician, his own inner psychic processes are blocked; he sees a distorted view of himself and may begin to live a lie to his patients. As long as he persists in denying his own wound - edness *he cuts off from himself an essential part of his healing power,* preferring to assuage his own ego rather than confront the shadowy elements that are a part of himself. He glues together this distorted view of himself with the element of power — personal power, his imagined notion of what healers should be like. He becomes a doer, for it is only through doing that he believes power can be wielded. This strategy transforms his patients into the recipients of his doing; and it is on 'the doing of the doctor' that cure and healing must hinge. He becomes a peddler of techniques; no matter that they are sophist - icated expressions of biotechnology, they are techniques none -

theless. And no matter that they occasionally seem to work, as they indeed do. What has occurred is that a deeper, more pro - found potential for healing and wholeness has been sacrificed.

How? *The patient becomes the sacrifice* – for in pro - jecting his own wounds onto the patient, the patient is further crippled. It is only the healer now who can save him through the incessant round of doing, of the endless wielding of technique. The stage is set for the "fix it" mode of medicine that has become the hallmark of our day.

The physician is an easy target in our time, but we should not forget that this scenario could not go on *but for the complicity of the patient.* It is the patient who allows the doctor's strategy to be enacted. After all, it fulfills a need for himself, too – for by repressing his own power, his own *inner healer,* the polarity of his own archetype, he escapes having to acknowledge that he is *the healthy wounded.* He can project his own inner healing power onto the physician, whose job it then becomes to do all the work. It is an escape of responsibility that the patient has engineered. He has become the genuine article: the helpless, woeful, innocent person who is stricken down by illness which he cannot possibly control, and who must, therefore, look to the source of power, the physician, to cure.

Most doctor-patient relationships are constituted along these lines. When a physician and a patient come together who have repressed, respectively, their woundedness and healthiness, a silent bargain is struck. The physician unconsciously agrees to de-emphasize the inner power of the patient in bringing about his own healing (he must reserve the power for himself, for it is only through this mechanism that he can disguise the fact of his own woundedness); and the patient silently agrees to not ac - knowledge his own power (to do so would create a respons - ibility for himself in getting well), not to point out the wounds of his healer (this would constitute such a threat that the entire relationship might crumble). In the context of such an agreement the average doctor-patient relationship limps along — sometimes working, sometimes not.

## An Alternative Approach to Transform the Doctor-Patient Relationship

What is the way out? The admission by the physician and the patient of the murky shadows within each — the woundedness of the healer and latent healthiness of the patient. Such a recog - nition would create the atmosphere wherein a new kind of healing could flower. It would entail no less than a radical transformation of the doctor-patient relationship.

> "The image of the wounded healer symbolizes an acute and painful awareness of sickness as the counterpole to the physician's health, a lasting and hurtful certainty of the degeneration of his own body and mind. This sort of experience makes the doctor the patient's brother rather than his master...
>
> In the final analysis [the physician] must always strive to constellate the healing factor in the patient. Without this he can accomplish nothing. An he can only truly activate this healing factor if he bears sickness as an existential possibility within himself. He is less effective when he tries to unite the two poles of the archetype through petty power."[9]

Thus a new vision of the doctor-patient relationship begins to take shape as both doctor and patient become attuned to the two poles of their archetype. The traditional hierarchical strat -

ification wherein the physician is seen as a powerful master directing the inner workings of the body of the subservient patient is transcended. This *does not mean* that in admitting his own woundedness the physician must actually take on the illness, for this would be a sentimental perversion of the recognition of weakness. And it *does not mean* that the patient, secure with the awareness of his own inner potential for healthiness, must never seek out a healer. For this, too, is an improper and shallow conclusion. The healing relationship goes beyond hierarchy, wherein neither healer nor the one to be healed stands above the other.

In the new context a basic humanism emerges, a quality that in the ordinary doctor-patient relationship is decidedly sup - pressed. Robert J. Sardello has described the flowering of this humanistic quality in speaking of the proper relationship be - tween teacher and student. Bearing in mind that the root meaning of the words "physician" and "teacher" is the same, Sardello's observations are keenly applicable to the doctor-patient relationship:

"When teaching and learning are imagined as a single action occurring for both teacher and student, a model of teaching more closely corresponding to the perennial pattern of the teacher is enacted. The teacher admits to being a student and students experience the desire to know awakened in their relationship with teachers. The teacher is touched by a certain vulnerability, is reminded over and over again that there is much that he does not know. He is deeply touched by students, excited, frightened, shaken by them. Only when the teacher is a perpetual learner does a learner desire knowledge. Like Chiron, whose very name refers to the hand and has connotations of touching with the hand, working by hand, practicing a handcraft or art, the teacher who allows himself to be touched, touches in turn."[10]

As Sardello has described the teaching-learning experience, the new vision of healing is that it is 'a single action.' Hier- archical differences, contingent on the wielding of power by one person over another, take a back seat. Power can be brought into play, *but it does not flow only from the doctor to the patient.* In full knowledge of the polarities within himself, the patient also uses power — this time on his own behalf, not content to let the doctor do it all. The appeal of the patient to the physician of "Fix it!" dissolves in the 'single action' of mutual effort.

This mode of interaction will suggest to some the im- possible. How can healing possibly occur as a "single action" unless a single person is involved? This sounds suspiciously like the mushy appeal to 'oneness' and 'sharing' and 'uniting' of the transpersonalist, who would have us, in effect, forget who we are, dissolving into some featureless relationship wherein one cannot tell doctor from patient or patient from doctor. We can't forget who we are and what we are, and this 'single action' mode of healing is nothing but words.

Yet the 'singleness' that we are speaking of is not a featureless blending of identities, a fusion of disparate qualities into some unrecognizable blur, but exactly the opposite. It is a mode of bringing about healing not through *forgetting* all the various qualities that make us who we are, *but in acknow- ledging them.* It is a new way of doing and being that becomes possible because we know *all* that we are. Because we now sense within us the shadows as well as the light, we are empowered into a new existential set of premises which say something entirely different about how healers and patients can interact and about how healing can come about.

Lewis Thomas once observed that, instead of always em- phasizing what we actually know in science, it would be enormously fruitful to focus alternatively on what we do *not* know. For it is here that the wonders lie. The known is the domain that is safe, where risk-taking is no longer necessary. To dwell in it forever is not only to never advance, it is also to promote a deceptive and false view of ourselves as knowing more than we do – of being more powerful than we really are.

I can conceive, too, that one day medical schools will emphasize not entirely the known, but a healthy dose of the unknown as well. It might give us not only a true picture of medical science, but also a truer vision of ourselves as well. It might remind us of something we have almost forgotten as modern physicians, and which we desperately need to remember: that first, and finally, and without exception, we are wounded healers.

**Notes:**
1 Robert J. Sardello, *Teaching as Myth in The Soul of Learning,* Pegasus Foundation Press, Dallas.
2 Adolf Guggenbühl-Craig, *Power in the Helping Professions,* Spring Publications, Inc., Dallas, 1982, p. 85.
3 ibid., p. 89.
4 ibid., p. 90.
5 Jerome Frank, "Mind-Body Relationships in Illness and Healing," *Journal of the International Academy of Preventative Medicine,* 2:3 (1975), pp. 46-59.
6 Larry Dossey, *Space, Time and Medicine,* Shambhala Publications, Boston, 1982 and Kenneth Pelletier, *Mind as Healer, Mind as Slayer,* Delta, New York, 1977.
7 *Power in the Helping Professions*, p. 91.
8 ibid.
9 *Power in the Helping Professions*, pp. 97, 100-101.
10 *Teaching as Myth*

# The AIDS Patient As Healer: A Case History

## by Niravi Payne

Every healer deeply committed to their own inner journey and self-growth process learns that there is no line separating healer from healee. They are interchangeable; not two distinct roles but a process evolving toward wholeness. In a reciprocal exchange of energy and love, healer and healee are one.

Patients who present themselves for treatment are in effect offering healers important opportunities to learn the lessons that life has in store for them. In working with clients, perhaps we are often speaking to parts of our own being to which we do not have easy access, because of our blinders of attachment or denial.

When we acknowledge that separateness is only an illusion; that we are one in this energy field of healing, we open ourselves to new possibilities of going beyond just treating symptoms. Healer and healee are "all in this together." Viewing the world from different perspectives, we may mirror each other, which again brings us back to ourselves, and gives us a chance to see who we really are. We are all children of life; some of us more conscious of this than others. Yet all of us are seeking a way to live more fully as ourselves.

Realization of this circular nature of the healing process

*Niravi Payne, M.S. is a founder and director of the Heights Holistic Health Association, an experienced psychotherapist, biofeedback specialist and group facilitator. She is a graduate of Hunter College, New York and a member of several professional associations. She is a frequent speaker to community groups and health care professionals. Before founding the Heights Holistic Health Association in 1978, she had 20 years experience in administrative, teaching, research and project development roles for various New York hospitals and health agencies.*

places an important responsibility on the healer to be as deeply committed to one's own search within as to the patient's search within. It involves summoning up the courage to face the darkness within, and the unregenerated parts of ourselves.

This makes our own openness, vulnerability, honesty, and feelings an integral part of the process of healing. Resistance on the part of a healer to dealing with one's own darkness will close off vital areas of exploration for the client. As we proceed to help our patients peel back multi-generational layers of negative conditioning, we are simultaneously going 'home' to the core of our own being, which needs healing. If we truly function as though there were no duality, the message of illness, its pur - pose, and meaning, all become an express train to that exquisite cutting edge of consciousness wherein lies the real awakening to our own nature and that of our clients.

This makes me aware that my work as a therapist is really my way of finding myself. The reason I am here is to remember who I really am and to help others get in touch with who they really are. My experiences with many clients make it graphically clear to me that my effectiveness as a healer requires an enormous commitment to downright caring for those I work with, a deep concern for what happens in the therapeutic pro - cess. It implies a willingness to explore beyond the parameters of psychotherapy and into spirituality.

The unknown is a powerful force for radical personal change. As we move into it, new potentials become accessible to us, and new possibilities and options emerge, out of which healing may take place. In this context the role of the healer is to encourage others to view life from a larger perspective and to learn to trust one's inner knowing.

At whatever level of consciousness healer and healee begin the journey, the exchange should move both closer to their heart center, wherein abides self-love and self-acceptance. Blame, judgments and misperceptions drop along the way. As healers serve as guides to clients, encouraging and urging them to trust and go beyond, so too, do clients become the healer's guide in a mutually strengthening exchange. Virginia Satir put it succinctly:

> "We are people dealing with people... We need to be able to understand and love ourselves, to be able to look, listen, touch and understand those we see. We need to be able to create the conditions by which we can be looked at, listened to, touched and understood."[1]

## The *Roots* of Illness

When a patient declares that they wish to be well, they often mean that they need to separate from the effects of generations of family psychodynamics. If they understood the depth of the work required to organically heal their bodies and their lives, most would run in the opposite direction! They wish to be well, yet want to maintain the connections to their parents' thinking, and with it the conditions which made them ill in the first place. This engenders tremendous fear of letting go of their whole identity. It invalidates the parent, who is supposed to be the source of love and acceptance.[2]

In our work we try to guide patients, in a spirit of loving encouragement, to feel safe enough to trust and go beyond the known − to new realms of consciousness, out of which true healing may emerge. The unknown, instead of being the enemy and a source of fear, then becomes a powerful force for permanent inner changes.

When we as healers touch the longing to be healed, free and well, we are also touching the deep-rooted fears and defenses that resist healing. All these resistances, often ingrained through many generations, lurk beneath the ostensible desire to be well, to frustrate and prevent healing. This paradox must be addressed in all healing processes.

## An Holistic Approach

The therapeutic basis for our work in psychosomatic therapy at the Heights Holistic Health Association rests on the following premises:

1) Illnesses don't just happen to us, but are an outgrowth out of our conflicted thoughts, feelings, beliefs, projections, atti - tudes, unexpressed emotions, behavior and attachments;

2) These early-learned emotional reactions to critical life events are linked to our childhood experiences and demonstrate how we replicate in our bodies multi-generational family patterns of illness;

3) These emotional reactions can suppress disease-fighting white blood cells and other elements of the immune system;

4) Learning how to make these vital connections can deci - sively affect the prevention and treatment of illnesses and the outcome of the healing process. Illness is an opportunity for healing, growth, freedom and life change;

5) Connecting one's mind and heart with the body may unlock the healing powers of the mind;

6) Beneath the verbal wish to be well lies a deep *resistance to healing* which we must learn to understand and respect.

In its infinite wisdom the body remembers what the mind wants to forget, either consciously or subconsciously. It serves us symptoms which are important messages from our inner self about ourselves, what we are living out from the past and what changes in our life need to be made now if we are to heal and be healthy.

In our experience we have found that these unresolved early childhood feelings are held in the body until a current situation of similar magnitude presents itself in a person's life. When the body can no longer sustain the pressure of a current conflict, it breaks through in the form of symptoms. We repeat through our symptoms a replication of past family history.

In our work at the Association we employ an integrative approach using psychotherapeutic interventions along with meditative practices, biofeedback, primal therapy, journal-keeping, drawing, visualization, and nutritional counseling to address the mental, emotional, physical, and spiritual needs of our clients. We seek to connect their present life with the effects of their early childhood conditioning, and assist them to go beyond their self-defeating, illness-provoking thoughts and behaviors, into a higher consciousness of healing:

> "The basic task of psychotherapy is to expand a person's sense of who he is by integrating the parts of himself that he treats as alien."[3]

> "If psychotherapy can heal the self-defeating splits between different parts within ourselves, meditation al- lows us to go one step further, by starting to dissolve the fortress of 'I,' and heal our split from life as a whole. Then a wider way of perceiving life can arise."[4]

> "Meditation provides an opportunity to directly experience how we keep trying to manufacture and hold onto a fixed identity as a defense against the uncertainties surrounding our lives."[5]

> "Yet, although therapy helps free a person from emotional and personal entanglements, it does not gener- ally provide a path for accessing or deepening the larger

sense of freedom and aliveness that arises in a moment of shift and opening, when old scripts and story-lines fall away."[6]

– John Wellwood

## Ray's Story

On January 14th, 1986, a very thin, young black man walked into the center and said: "My name is Ray...I have AIDS...will you work with me?" I hurriedly agreed, we shook hands, made an appointment, and he left.

As he walked out the door I suddenly confronted my unrealized fear of AIDS. That fear of death and illness was still there in me, despite what I teach and personally practice about the role of the mind and emotions in disease.

I washed my hands, the door knob, and...began another step in my own inner journey as a healer! His subsequent process of healing profoundly affected his own life, myself as his therapist, and the majority of my clients.

Ray was recovering from a recent hospital stay for pneumocystocitis. He began coming in twice a week, and a picture emerged of the things he had trouble dealing with: homosexuality, questions posed to him about his sexuality, his stressful job situation, loss of contact with his father and siblings for over a year, and the loss of his mother at the age of 36 to lung disease. He was surprised to become ill. He had taken very good care of his body with a commitment to proper nutrition, aerobics and yoga, but as he put it: "My personal life is a mess." He was drinking, and subject to feelings of self-hatred and self-destruction. He had been in therapy some time before, but had terminated treatment when he began working on issues around his father.

He had not had much to do with his father until his last hospital stay, when his father began calling him on a daily basis, "telling me he loved me, something he has never told me before. I thought he hated me. Before this he would never give me a chance."

Ray's father was muscular, overweight, athletic and broad, priding himself on his macho stance toward the world, particularly toward women. Ray was his firstborn son, named after him, but not at all what his father expected: he turned out to be a frail and sickly child. Ray's mother gave him a nickname which he bitterly resented: "BooBoo." "Nothing I do can make my dad like me...Dad I really want you to like me...I really do. 'I want you to like me, you son of a bitch'. I'd forgotten a lot of that pain; I never got angry or raised my voice, I was afraid to. But when I see his face I still feel fear. I'm beginning to see the similarities [to my dad] in the men I've picked as partners. All this rage is new and I don't know how to handle it."

When I asked Ray, "Why do you want to live," he summed up his conflict as follows: "...because I feel I am an instrument of love. I live off my interactions with others. I like people, but I am extremely judgmental. I give them the best part of me but I will take it back, too." He had such a need to be taken care of that he had married, as a way out of his misery. But that failed. He had a son he had never seen, repeating his father's treatment of him.

Ray initially spoke of his mother as someone he liked a lot and felt that "...she really liked me as a person." However, as we worked together, he began to get in touch with feelings of anger he had suppressed towards her. She had married his father at the age of 15, had six children, and died at the age of 36 of alcoholism and pneumonia. She could not handle parenting, was provocative and controlling, and "took charge of everything from a couch." She would often instigate his father to beat Ray with a strap for the slightest infraction. She had Ray doing all the housework for the entire family. When she left the house she would lock all the children in a closet "for safekeeping." Ray spoke of his parents as "taking out a lot of anger on all of us and, in particular, they could not handle me." Ray's father left his mother for another woman when Ray was 14 years old, and his mother fell apart.

If there was to be any healing it was essential that Ray see that what he was living out in his illness was connected with his early childhood conditioning and family psychophysical dynamics. He could then examine what needed changing in order for his life to function with love, health, joy and self-respect.

Given my understanding of the psychodynamics of illness I felt it was essential that Ray see that the seeds of his illness were sown in the years of early childhood abuse, verbal and physical, and not just in the parental reactions to his being gay. Therapy which examines only current parental rejections of homo - sexuality in a child, and condemns the patient to regard this factor as the only basis for their inner conflicts, deprives them of much of the basis for understanding the other factors in their relationships. If Ray saw this as a gay issue only, he would stay stuck in self-hate, self-denigration and self-punishment. He would continue to use his illness both as a means of getting attention, and retaliation against his father for rejecting him, using his own life as the instrument of punishment.

This need to be taken care of was unusually deep-seated and pervasive in Ray. It was unsurprising, given his history of neglect, abandonment and abuse by both parents. During the early stages of the disease, Ray had stayed home from work to see if he could fight off the fevers, but alone at home he felt abandoned by everyone. This changed to relief upon hospitalization, as he felt he was at last "getting taken care of."

After discharge, however, all contact with his father ended, as did much support from his friends.

Looking at the metaphysical causes of AIDS we find, as with all illnesses, a denial of the self and a strong belief in not being good enough. Central to Ray's healing process was a need to move to a place of self-love. But he was burdened with hundreds of constantly reinforced messages from his parents: "...you are bad, you are not good enough, you are not worth anything, the older you get the dumber you get...": a heavy load to carry!

Through gestalt and primal therapy, we helped Ray mobilize his unexpressed anger at his parents' treatment of him, the loss of his mother at such a young age, his father's rejections of him, the loss of contact with his family, and his desperate need for acceptance by his father and siblings. "The realization that there is so much rage in me is very scary; but at the same time I'm also realizing that the whole family was a very frightened family."

As Ray expressed anger at his mother, he also got in touch with his guilt feelings about her death: "I accepted her drinking and it killed her. I feel it is my fault. I resented my stubborn - ness and turned it in on myself." During one therapy session, as his anger mounted at his mother, he shouted at her, shaking a pillow, "Wake up!...sitting there drinking all day...I cannot carry your burden on my shoulders...it is not my problem. I don't want to confuse the life part of me with the dead part of you, mother!"

An essential element in our therapy was the need for Ray to experience the interconnection between his mind, body and emotions in the healing process. Through the use of the thermo - gram, a biofeedback instrument for measuring fluctuations in skin temperature, Ray could actually experience how his thoughts and feelings influenced his bodily reactions: when holding back, denying, not wanting to know and not wanting to confront, his body temperature would go down. When he would connect with the underlying issues, he would release his tension and his skin temperature would go up. When he re - pressed his rage, anger and disappointment with his boss, friends, lovers, etc., he would wind up with a mouth full of thrush. When he openly expressed his feelings, his mouth was clear, he was less bothered by fevers, his symptoms abated, his body felt stronger and his appetite increased.

It was difficult for Ray to come to terms with the enormity of the abuse and damage inflicted upon him since his very early childhood. As he got more in touch with the reality of his parents' abusive behavior, he said, "I did not deserve this...it was a terrible injustice."

Over the first seven months of counseling Ray, I had to confront my own fears of death, and acknowledge that we do not have to die because of the past. I said to him: "Go out because of *your own* dynamic, not because you are living out your early childhood hell." I began to believe that it was possible to turn any illness, including AIDS, into a healing experience; that Ray did not have to die if he worked hard enough; that I would not have to die either as my parents did; as Ray was making it, so was I. His remaining alive affirmed the power of my work.

## Family Reconstruction

A profound change occurred in Ray in March 1986, when I invited him to participate in a weekend therapy marathon which I run every six weeks for all of my clients. Modeled after Virginia Satir's work, the weekend is a powerful therapeutic and learning experience for all participants. A member of the group selects other members of the group to play themselves and their family. Called "family reconstruction," it is a dramatic re-enactment of childhood, the parents' and grandparents' families, and the impact on their life today. Illuminating past events and connecting them with present feelings paves the way for new learning. Outmoded ways of coping with life become evident.

"Family reconstruction is a powerful, dramatic exper - ience that enables us to make discoveries about our families and our psychological learnings of our child - hood, but often they no longer fit our present context. By revisiting the sources of these old learnings, we can look at them with new eyes and discard those that create problems for us."[7]

Seeing *yourself* onstage in relationship to members of your immediate family is often very painful. Old family patterns of isolation, disconnection, rejection, and loneliness re-emerge. The vividness of the experience is described by Michele Baldwin:

"One advantage of sculpting is that, as a behavioral demonstration, it is much more accurate in what it reflects about family communications than a verbal description. Another advantage is that it makes past experiences alive in the present."[8]

This process created close bonding and sharing among the group, as they all became mothers and fathers, sisters and brothers, etc. for each other. A therapeutic community slowly developed, with each participant committed to the healing of self and others. During the weekend I asked the group if they would allow Ray to join in this *sculpting* process.

I don't think I or anyone who participated that day can forget the incredible reaction to Ray's announcement to his "mother" during the process: "Mother, I have AIDS and I am dying." A palpable shock ran through the 26 other participants, but it was not until the evening wrap-up that their collective fear, rage, anger and feelings of betrayal exploded at me: "How could you have done such a thing without asking us first! How could you endanger the lives of everyone here!" and so forth. During this time it was essential for me to remain calm and centered within, as this reactive phase is a vital part of the healing process.

An honest, open battle was waged for Ray's place in this "family" as they openly expressed their feelings and fears about death with Ray present. He re-experienced his family's unexpressed voices of rejection and disapproval. But openly expressed, we were able together to work through to a place of acceptance and caring, something Ray had never been able to do with his own family.

We were all pushed to the farthest edge, beyond the para - meters of what was acceptable, and we all grew. By mid-weekend integration and inclusion occurred, warm and loving feelings were opened, and Ray became a family member. The bonding increased further as Ray was asked to play members of the family of other participants. This experience of confronting death, and the struggle to live, made everyone aware that the two are inseparable. It became a powerful healing force that trans - formed Ray into a healer, as he fought not only for his own existence, but for the quality of life of all involved. His very presence caused each person present to examine and re-examine their prejudices and judgments, as well as their capacity to open to and expand the risk-taking, flexible, health-giving aspects of their nature.

Flowing from the weekend experience I decided to have Ray join the weekly group which forms the core base of the larger weekend marathons. Despite their weekend experience, this request again raised fears about death and illness among many of the group members. Also, they had begun to feel close to Ray and, remembering grief at the loss of their own family members, felt they could not endure the pain should Ray "not make it." Other issues of prejudice against gays also came up.

It took two weekly sessions before the group finally agreed, again learning and growing in the process of challenging their own fears and limitations. Ray became a full member of the "family." His perceptiveness grew as his defensiveness was challenged and as he openly challenged others.

Ray began to gain weight, health and strength, returning to work, first part-time then full-time. He was given increased responsibility on the job. He felt stronger and stronger. He looked terrific. He began fixing up his apartment and buying new furniture. As he improved, we began to believe that he could indeed come through this serious challenge to health and life.

## Hearing the Inner Message

Yet, even in this ostensibly positive framework, as Ray expressed his excitement at being healthy, the thermogram he was attached to registered a sharp drop in his skin temperature. He was astounded at this demonstration of his fear of giving up his illness. The link was becoming clearer to him between sickness and his need for constant emotional support. Drawing up a detailed family tree, he commented: "I am a part of this family, and when I get very ill – close to death – then everyone comes to me and tries to help me and keep me alive."

When ill, he could throw it in his father's face: "Look what you did to me," hoping to find some concern, some expression of caring, as had occurred during his previous hospitalizations. By getting well, he would be giving up his opportunity to punish his father and his need to punish himself. Therapists often pay too little attention to this paradox: people are, on the surface, fighting to get healthy, yet at the same time they have a need to stay ill. The illness is their connection with parental conditioning. Getting well means separating from this, and a sundering of self from their idealized parents. This recognition is an extremely painful one, not readily welcomed. The patient may be maintaining an illness because of the underlying belief that any connection is better than none.

In the group, Ray received attention for the opposite reason: for fighting for his life, to change, to grow, to live and be healthy.

At one of the Thursday night groups, Dorothy, who rarely participated and when she did was rather inaudible, recounted the story of her twin sister dying at their birth. Her mother had withheld this information from her for 15 years. As Ray heard Dorothy, he suddenly looked at her sad and pinched face and said, "You feel guilty just for being alive! You have just as much right to live as the concentration camp survivors!" She began to weep, finally admitting to herself that her mother was still mourning the dead twin, ignoring her and blaming her for living! It was an important breakthrough for her. Ray certainly knew what it felt like to feel guilty for living.

In early February, 1987, Ray began to face serious conflicts in his life. He received an unfavorable evaluation from his boss, and again re-experienced his old feelings of rejection by a father figure.

At about the same time, his lover was contemplating going to Ireland, which brought up old feelings of rejection. This caused new trauma, as it conflicted with his desperate need for approval. He began to see how like his mother he was in his interrelationships, which caused further pain.  The periods of high body temperature began to return.  His emotional and phys - ical condition began to deteriorate markedly.  He began to think he might not make it, and began to look haggard, thinner and weaker.  It became apparent that the disease, despite all our efforts to stem the tide, was gaining control when threatened by the larger fears of rejection and abandonment.  Human beings seem willing to pay whatever price is necessary to feel loved, to belong, to feel as if they matter, even if the price exacted is illness and death.  This was at the heart of Ray's struggle.

As I saw his condition deteriorate I felt a chill of repulsion go through me: "If you are not going to live, go away. I can't face the possibility of your death. I don't want to feel a failure, nor a threat to my ability to keep myself healthy."  Before I could be totally present for him I had to do some soul-searching as I worked through these feelings.

Ray was with me for a therapy session on February 16, 1987. That same night he became critically ill and was admitted to the hospital. The following evening, our group met to discuss visiting him and once again all were thrown into turmoil as they grappled with their renewed fear of AIDS and of death, and the possibility of losing Ray, who they had all come to love and respect.  Group members who had distanced themselves from their own families found themselves face to face with the feel - ings which the conflict around Ray had stirred up.  It unmasked many unexpressed fears and feelings about loss, illness and dying.

One by one, each member of the smaller group as well as the larger one went to the hospital, until the constancy of the visits astounded the floor staff.  Flowers, plants, balloons, cards, drawings, reflexology and Reiki treatments, and other expres - sions of love and support poured into the hospital room. Through Ray we began to face our fears of death, loss and intimacy. All spurned the prescribed masks and gloves, feeling that these prevented quality contact. Ray lay shivering on ice mattresses to bring his raging fevers down, clutching his oxygen mask tightly to his nose and mouth, although it was already secured firmly by a strong rubber strap. I was reminded of the little boy who sucked air from underneath the door when locked in a closet with his siblings by his mother.

As we witnessed his struggle, we realized how we take our breathing for granted, as well as our opportunity to live and be. We realized how much we loved him and respected both him and ourselves for overcoming much of our narrowness in order to learn how to give. It became apparent that our trips to the hospital were as much for ourselves as for Ray.

During one visit, he was given an original drawing by another member of the group. Noticing it was unsigned, he insisted that she sign it. In many similar ways he offered people recognition and authentication of themselves.

When Ray was first hospitalized I called his father in Pittsburgh, urging him to see Ray. He did respond a few days later, only to stand by the hospital door, stay a few minutes, and leave. The next morning Ray told me of the pain he felt at his father's coldness. I obtained his permission to visit his father and sisters, who were staying in Ray's apartment. I went to see his family, wondering how I would reach them with the urgent need for them to really connect with Ray. I felt incredibly awkward, yet I felt it was critical for Ray that I break through. They seemed distant and remote. Finally I broke down and cried, and said: "I'm only Ray's therapist and I love him! He is your son and he needs to feel your love. For God's sake, if not now, when? You can't hug a wooden box! You need to speak some words of healing while you still have someone to say them to!" Somehow what I said got through to them. We were all crying. Ray's father said, "What can I do?" I said, "Just hold him, hug him and tell him that you love him."

I visited Ray the next day and he greeted me with: "Wow! It was like having a new father."

One visit I found Ray in great pain from what seemed like indigestion. He had been afflicted with similar pain before, for hours on end. As we worked together on the meaning of his pain, he suddenly realized that it represented his continuing conflict with his mother, and the need to let her go. The pain ended immediately. He smiled his relief and so did I.

By mid-March Ray had rallied to the point where the physicians were considering discharging him in a week or so and making plans for visiting nurses and meals at home. They were astounded by his acceptance by heterosexuals. He was called the "miracle patient" for fighting his way back against all the odds. Ray was elated. He spoke of buying a red car as soon as he was fully well.

But as he recovered, his apprehension of going home was rising. For in the hospital he was cared for, while at home he felt very much alone. As he got better, the frequency of visits by members of the group declined. The old fears of aban - donment began to reassert themselves. He became angry at me for not coming as frequently as before. I was feeling worn down, and I felt I had lost the *boundaries* of a therapist. I became deeply concerned because once again he was being rewarded for being ill, but not for healing. This feeds a root cause of illness: the need to get attention and to be cared for.

When I walked into his hospital room after an interval of two days, I was shocked to see him semi-comatose. It seemed that the virus had suddenly invaded his brain.

At that point, it was incredibly painful for me to look down into his sparkling black eyes. In a spirit of forgiveness, love and completion, I held him and talked about his preparing to leave for another level of being. His eyes remained very clear, speaking words his lips could not release.

He died on March 26, 1987.

It was a Thursday, the night our weekly group met. In pain and grief, we talked together, cried together, and explored our deep and pervasive fear of dying. We struggled to gain a larger perspective on the unity of life and death as one process and the healing spirit that Ray had catalyzed in all of us. We realized we could not re-create Ray, or hold on to our experience of him, rather than live in the present moment with all its unknown newness.

The memorial service that Saturday was attended by his father, a sister, and many members of his extended therapeutic family, as well as his lover, his boss and his co-workers. As they spoke I asked myself what I could say publicly, knowing Ray so much more intimately after all our work together. I chose to remain silent, communing with Ray's spirit, and meditating on all he had taught me about healing, humility, ego and genuine, courageous loving.

We later considered these words by Krishnamurti:

"Most of us are frightened of dying because we don't know what it means to live. We don't know how to live and therefore we don't know how to die... As long as we are frightened of life we shall be frightened of death. The person who is not frightened of life is not frightened of being completely insecure, for they understand that inwardly, psychologically, there is no security. When there is no security there is endless movement, and then life and death are the same. The person who lives with - out conflict, who lives with beauty and with love, is not frightened of death. If you die to everything you know including your family, your memories, everything you have felt then death is a purification, a rejuvenating process. To find out what actually takes place when you die, you must die...not physically, but psychologically: inwardly die to the things you have cherished and are bitter about. If you have died to one of your pleasures, the smallest or the greatest, naturally and without any enforcement or argument, then you will know what it means to die. To die is to have a mind that is completely empty of itself, empty of its daily longings, pleasures and agonies. When there is death there is something totally new. Freedom from the known is death – and then you are living."9

Unless we as healers are willing to confront our own pain and darkness, we can never be truly open to that joining of energy with our patients that is necessary for the fullest healing process to take place for both.

In Alice Miller's advice to a therapist in training, she says, "First try to discover your own childhood, then take the exper - ience seriously... Try to feel, and help the patient to feel... study the history of childhood... Therapy has to open you as well as the patient for feeling in your life. It has to awaken you from a sleep."10

Ray's transition was a most profound experience of self-discovery of the depth of love in healing, of overcoming fears and limitations, and confronting the exquisite interrelationship of life/death as one process. I had to learn that success and failure in the healing experience was not predicated on whether the person lived and was healed, or died. It is not what happens at the end of the road, but the quality of the experience as we move along, that is important. What I also learned is that loss isn't only about losing people we love, but about losing illusions about ourselves as people and as healers:

"Health is not equivalent to happiness, surfeit, or suc -
cess. It is foremost a matter of being wholly one with
whatever circumstances we find ourselves in. Even our
death is a healthy event if we fully embrace the fact of
our dying... The issue is awareness, of living in the
present. Whatever our present existence consists of, if
we are at one with it, we are healthy."[11]

**Notes:**

1  Virginia Satir &Michele Baldwin, *Satir Step By Step,*
   Science and Behavior Books, Inc., Palo Alto, 1983.
2  Daniel Goleman, *Clues to Behavior Sought in History of
   Families,* New York Times Science Times, Jan 21, 1986.
3  John Wellwood, Ed., *Awakening the Heart:
   East/West Approaches To Psychotherapy,*
   Shambhala Publications, Boston, 1983, p. 46.
4  ibid, p. 47.
5  ibid, p. 47.
6  ibid, p. 48.
7  *Satir Step By Step,* p. 237.
8  *Satir Step By Step,* p. 244.
9  From a taped reading by Joseph Goldstein,
   *Opening To Fear,* Insight Meditation Center, Barre, MA.
10 Alice Miller, "Violence: Alice Miller's Impact on
   Psychotherapy," *The Common Boundary,* Vol. 5, Issue 3,
   May/June 1987.
11 Mwalimu Imara, *Dying As the Last Stage Of Growth,* as
   quoted from Death: The Final Stage of Growth, Elizabeth
   Kubler-Ross, Prentice-Hall, Inc., Englewood Cliffs, N.J.,
   1975, p. 147.

# The Mystic Unity of Healing

## by Andrew Vidich

The ancient Greek philosopher Herodotus once said, "call no man happy till you see how he meets his end." For Herodotus, no less than for us today, death was the mirror in which man's elemental nature was revealed. Virtually every human being has to face the death of a close friend or relative at least once in their lifetime. Yet for all its unavoidable pervasiveness, in Western culture death has ceased to be accepted as a meaningful or even natural phenomenon. Witnesses to death have been culturally conditioned to react with shock and dismay to the sight of a loved one on their death bed. It is as if all meaning and sense were stripped from reality, and man "is no more than a bare forked animal."[1]

Death seems to come upon us like a thief in the night, robbing us of both our humanity and individuality in one fell swoop. In the stark and brutal reality of death, the very roots of culture and civilization are shaken. For most people, the event of death is the most untimely, unwelcome and feared moment in one's life.

During the last epoch, death has been deritualized, sanitized, and removed from the warm and congenial atmosphere of the home to the cold and sterile hospital ward. The attitude of the doctor has been to see death as a business loss or "failure." In an

*Andrew Vidich is currently completing a Ph.D. in cultural anthropology. He has worked for over 10 years with the terminally ill. He teaches at growth centers, hospitals, conferences, colleges and peace organizations throughout the Northeast. He has authored numerous articles and poems. Andrew currently teaches workshops on 'Conscious Living & Conscious Dying,' and is public relations coordinator for Science of Spirituality in New York. He seeks to integrate the principles of individual transformation into a contemporary context of healing. He lives with his wife and son in Staten Island, New York.*

ironic reversal of roles, it is now the doctor instead of the priest who "claims control of death as his mission in life."[2] The acceptable death is one in which the dying person "passes away" in his sleep, or simply doesn't wake up. With the advent of technology, death is seen as an accident or illness that must be brought under control at all costs. Death has become a calculated event, outside the control of the individual who is dying. This approach is represented by the "total bureaucratization and management of death" under the auspices of the hospital. Even the natural event of mourning has been relegated to funeral directors who have assumed the role of "doctors of grief."[3] Death, dying, and even the aging process have become cruel symbols for "evil nature" and a retreat from normal society.

In recent years, beginning as early as 1959, when Herman Feifel wanted to interview the dying, perhaps for the first time in our era, the hospital authorities responded with indignation. As Philipe Aries notes, they found the project "cruel, sadistic, and traumatic."[4] Some years later, when Elizabeth Kubler-Ross was looking for dying persons to interview, the heads of hospitals and clinics protested: "Dying? But there are no dying here."[5] Indeed, not only had death been fully "tamed," but entirely *evacuated*.

By 1969, a collective anthology entitled *The Dying Patient*, boasted a bibliography of over 340 titles in English collected since 1955 on the subject of dying.[6] The massive interest evidenced by the surge of recent publications, was spear-headed by the work of Dr. Kubler-Ross. In her book, *On Death and Dying,* she sought not only to ameliorate the actual process of dying, but to restore to the dying person his forgotten dignity. Some years later, Stephen Levine reintroduced in his book, *Who Dies,* the age-old spiritual concept of a "conscious death." Drawing from the Hindu and Buddhist philosophers, he sought to examine death in light of a spiritual transformation.[7] Although the work of Dr. Kubler-Ross had a profound impact in bringing the issues of death and dying to the American public, little effort has been made to introduce the patient to a meaningful experience of these concepts.

The great irony of our culture is that, despite our significant advancements in technology and psychology, we still remain more primitive than our ancestors in dealing with death.[8] We are essentially powerless and helpless when confronted with the brutality and finality of death. Death in many ways is the great 'angst' of culture because we have failed to provide the dying with a sense of the 'eternal,' or what poets and mystics have called the "logos vision."[9]

In the West, the experience of the eternal has been relegated to a post-mortem existence. Christians tend to speak of "eternal life" as something that only begins after you die physically, divorcing our present life from the life hereafter. In this way we bury the spirit along with the corpse and the survivors await death without preparation or understanding. It is in this sense that "Christianity is the religion of fallen man" for it has ceased to generate a continuous experience of the eternal for those who are still alive.[10]

Death is not merely a single moment marking the biological end of life. Death is the grand mirror in which the totality of our life is reflected. The great fear of death with which our society is stricken is in reality the fear of ourselves. Rumi, the great mystic poet of Sufism, was reported to have said, "Your fear of death is really your fear of yourself: see what it is you are fleeing from."[11] It is not death, then, which is the pathology, but rather the act of living.

As we look into the "mirror of death" we see ourselves clearly, as if through a magic glass. As the menace of death approaches, man stands in all his nakedness and horror, awe - somely revealed to himself. Death allows no hypocrisy: the inner

man can no longer hide under a cloak of piety. One can con -
veniently forget others' deaths, one may even romanticize them,
but our own death clutches at our very being. Indeed, the pro -
cess of death represents not only a chemical return to nature –
"from dust thou cometh and to dust returneth" – but a psychic
and spiritual return as well.

Nature seeks a balance, and neither suppression nor
repression is of any value in the face of the volcanic eruptions
released by the psyche at the time of death. The psyche, as Carl
Gustav Jung has argued, seeks a harmonious balance between
its inner unconscious existence and the conscious life of the
outer personality. Though we may think and act in defiance of
the inner psyche, it is fully aware of who and what we are. The
psyche, like death, acts as a mirror and reflects back to us
through our own dreams, "death's second self," what the best
counseling fails to achieve.

Recent historical studies of death have revealed the extent to
which ancient cultures were aware of the need for an "Ars
Morienenda," or "art of dying." This art of dying was embodied
not only in the religious texts, but also in literature and myths. In
many of the eschatological mythologies, not only were detailed
descriptions of the afterlife states of mind or abodes of the
deceased given, such as heaven, paradise or hell, but also they
offered precise cartographies to guide the dying through the
sequential changes of consciousness that "occur during the
critical period of transition."[12] This art of dying was not
acquired through intellectual study, but through an intense
training period in which the student was taught to encounter
death before the actual demise of the body. During these
"symbolic deaths," a profound and shattering experience of
spiritual rebirth occurs, altering any previously held notions of
death or dying. It is this "initiatory death" which lies at the core

of most esoteric traditions: the "ascent of the shaman" to the higher world.[13]

The notion of a spiritual rebirth precipitated by an "initiatory death" has, as does death, both a psychological as well as symbolic meaning. If we assume that death and birth are correlative terms, every change of state "is both a death and a birth, depending on the side it is envisaged from."[14] In quite the same way the "art of dying" is also the "art of living." The pictorialized version of this art is exemplified as heaven and hell. In the former, life is envisioned as a state of perfect freedom and paradisical enjoyment. In the latter, hell is the personification of suffering which has its roots in "craving" or illusory existence. On the one side, there is the bondage of an individual existence fragmented from the whole and on the other the "beautific vision," or "void of no thing" (pure existence). There is in man, as the Great Buddha said, something which must die or which must be destroyed, and that is "craving" or "desire." In this cosmic play of opposites the drama of self unfolds against the backdrop of time. And it is thus that death represents, at any given moment in this drama, the degree to which we have embraced "reality" or "illusion." It is by "making stepping stones of our dead selves, until we realize at last that there is literally nothing to which we can identify our Self, that we can become *what we are*."[15]

The sundering of spirit from flesh represents not only the "dark night of the soul" mentioned in all esoteric traditions, but also, more importantly, the union of individual consciousness with cosmic consciousness. Angelus Silesius was reported to have said "What though I die hourly, I have each time found a better life."[16] It is the death of self or ego which precipitates the birth of the cosmic "I" or God-consciousness. Death, like the individual soul, at the primordial level cannot be differentiated from life. Even on the biological level every new breath brings the death of millions of cells and the birth of millions more.

The practice then, for those who would heal themselves or presume to work with the dying, is not an outward motion, but an inward attunement to this dying of self on all levels. One can be of no use to others unless and until one's own place is firmly planted in the awareness of one's own bondages and limitations. One important step in this journey of the healer and the healed occurs when there is the constant readiness to forgive the past. This experience re-enacts the "burying of the dead" and birth of "healing into life" which are mutually interdependent. Forgive - ness seen in this light is an inner action toward ourselves first and then outwardly to others. Compassion or "feeling with" arises out of the shared experience of common grief. But true empathy for the other arises from the experience of self-less- ness: awareness in which the bounds and limitations of individu - ality are completely shattered. When the ego dies, completely pure or primordial compassion is born. From this perspective there is neither healer nor healed, neither "I" nor "other," but only the vastness of consciousness itself mirroring its own light.

Some fifteen years ago my mother became close friends with a man named Charles, who was black and an alcoholic. Charles was born and raised in Harlem and by the time he was thirteen he had already tasted the worst of life. He was a problem alcoholic. During the time he lived with us he seemed to become worse and worse. As his dependency on my mother increased, so did her concern and attachment. He was subject to unpredict - able outbreaks of violence, rage and catatonic depression.

One weekend a seven year old boy named Elton and his mother were visiting our family. Charles had gone on a drinking binge, after which he got in a car along with Elton and another man and went on a joyride. About an hour later we received a call from the local hospital to say that that Charles had hit another car head on. The caller went on to say that one person was dead, and the child, Elton, critically wounded. Charles and the other driver were alive, but very seriously hurt.

The child was brutally injured. He suffered severe damage to his face and body. He hung on to life despite a host of broken bones and disfiguring wounds. Although he escaped with his life, the doctors feared he would either be crippled or horribly scarred or both. For many days he was unconscious or incoherent. When we finally were able to see him after about two weeks of anxious waiting, our nerves were ragged. The whole family felt a crushing sense of guilt for having allowed Charles such an opportunity.

When I walked in to the hospital room I was immediately impressed by the extent of the child's recovery. Little Elton was wide-eyed, bright, and smiling. Although he had all sorts of tubes and needles going in and out of his body, he was able to speak and move his head to the left and right. I was immediately struck by his incredible resilience and courage. He was clearly quite cheerful and happy. Though his physical body remained contorted and distorted, his spirit still shone with its youthful luster and brilliance; indeed it shone even brighter than before. As I sat in the room I was simultaneously revolted and awestruck: revolted by the brutal disfiguration and awestruck by his unassuming beauty and courage.

The two apparently contradictory impressions made me cry. There was something incompatible, which I found difficult to digest. I remember feeling extremely fortunate to be alive. But this thought bothered me: here was this mangled boy who might never recover completely from this accident, which on the surface seemed unjust and meaningless, I could only think of myself! I began to see, as I stared at the boy's smiling face, how cruel and insensitive my reactions really were. I was not relating to his needs or even sharing in a simple way that moment with him. I was blinded by the vision of my own death and the apparent meaninglessness of his pain.

But as I stood looking at the child, my emotions changed again. Instead of fear and revulsion, I began to see the beauty of the child's spirit. Instead of pity, I felt only the deepest love and reverence. Instead of being revolted by his physical appearance, I began to see his buoyant spirit in all its pristine glory.

Our family left, but something in me stayed in that room. Something died during those moments. I realized for the first time the power of death as a healing medium. This child had touched the face of death and was robust with life. And by merely looking into this boy's shining spirit I was also able to confront my own death vicariously. In that recognition was the transition from a view of death as being gruesome and hateful, to one in which it was spiritually renewing and healing. I began to see my own emotions of fear and pain in their own light. They were the extensions of my own selfish ego and contracted self. This boy was healed because he was in the healing presence of his spirit. He was in the present and open to the moment despite the mass of broken bones and scars. He was healed instantly because he had no regrets, guilt, or attachment to his body.

This child and many other children who face death at an early age, seem to be profound examples of the "healing model." Still shining with the radiance of their inner life, they are, as Wordsworth has said, "the father of man." In their uncorrupted state of innocence there is a purity which is "healing person - ified." It is their *whole* spirit which brings them healing and their healing in turn restores them to greater *wholeness*.

Charles, the driver, also recovered, but not for a long period of time. Even after his hospital confinement he remained men - tally and physically handicapped. Like little Elton, he was lucky to have lived at all. Even after his physical recovery his spirit was plagued with the terrible guilt and responsibility of his past actions. Unable to face this pain he resorted to heavy drinking once again. No one could share his unique world of guilt, self-hatred and devastation. No one could touch for him the "healing presence" of his own spirit.

Four painful years after the car accident he became seriously ill with cirrhosis of the liver. The doctor's prognosis was extremely poor: a 30% chance of survival. The ultimatum finally came: stop drinking or face death.

During this hospital stay I came to visit him. For the first time in years he was sober, alert, and communicative. The street jive was gone and a simple and humble Charles I had never before known stood before me. We instantly connected on the level of spirit. We talked about many things. Both of us knew something very deep had happened. He had decided he was not going to write his own death notice. He had accepted the challenge of changing his life and dwelling in the living present. For the first time there was the willingness to face the respons - ibility of his own actions. The past was dead, and with it the history of useless self-castigation and self-hatred. All the years of lecturing on my part had been futile. It was clear that nothing my mother or I had done previously to try to *heal* or *help* Charles had had any value. The moment was full, with a silent poignancy. Sharing this mutual recognition, both of us felt a deep healing occur. The years of dialogue in which I was the *helper* and he the *helped* seemed a distant dream. We both realized the futility of trying to change someone from without.

No one changes until they are profoundly moved from within to do so. There can be no healing moment until there is a realization of personal wholeness, which is nothing less than drawing from the spirit our essential nature, an experience which is beyond the limitations of "I" and "other." The experience of "I" and "other" is the experience of duality and is already

removed from the spirit, which recognizes no such boundaries. In my case, I realized one does not *heal* unless one transcends the role of healer. In Charles' case, it was the realization that one cannot blame the universe or oneself; one can only *act* appropriately in the present moment, true to one's highest vision. For my mother it was the realization that sometimes the greatest disservice is rendered by trying to remove the *obstacle* which is blocking this healing moment from occurring.

That obstacle is in fact the *gift* which ultimately leads to the healing moment. To remove it is to weaken the spirit further. While present, it offers us an ever-present opportunity to rise above it. In Zen there is a saying, "The greater the obstacle, the greater the gain." Often in our attempt to hasten or hurry the process we do immeasurable harm. The time factor is always there, but the moment we face death with openness, the healing moment is close at hand.

The entire journey of the healer and the healed is a foretaste of the experience of the "Eros vision" or lover-beloved relation - ship. With each successive step toward union, the lover must symbolically and literally die to his or her own individuality. In the medieval myth *Parcifal,* it is the "youth made wise through compassion" who is able to heal the ailing King Anfortas of his incurable wound. It is the holy sword, which represents the death of desire, which alone is able to heal the King. In a similar way there can be no union without annihilation of desire. In the lane of love two separate beings cannot exist together. So long as there is a lover and a beloved, union is impossible. In precisely the same way, the ontological explanation for death is the same as love. There is grief, mourning, death and decay because there is matter, mind, ego and individuality. As the veils of duality are removed, love reveals itself as the only true healer, since it mirrors the essence of God. The curative presence of love alone can restore the unitive state of the soul "so that it may behold the face of the fair," as Rumi so eloquently put it.

From the Druids we learn that "death is the center, not the finish of a long life."[17] For those who would seek healing, let them make death the pivot around which turns the axis of life. In response to the statement of Herodotus, Sant Kirpal Singh, a mystic of the 20th century, has said "those who have learnt to die meet death with greater happiness than on their own marriage day." The grief of the dying then is not on account of death; it is because they have dwelt on the phenomenal forms of existence. And courage, as the Greek philosopher Plotinus suggested, "is fearlessness in the face of death which is but the parting of the soul from the body."[18] He who has forgotten the eternal while in the temporal sees neither beloved nor eternity, but the abyss of extinction.

Unfortunately, the preparation for death in our present day culture affords the dying with little more than a mass of test tubes and nervous doctors who themselves find death savage and brutal. In recent years this has been ameliorated by the birth of the hospice movement which has sought to reestablish a meaningful context in which the dying may live their remaining days.

This new treatment of the dying, though beneficial in itself, cannot replace what only the individual himself must face, i.e. his own mortality. In this context, there can be no *treatment* for the dying because death is not something which is treated. On the contrary, death seems to provide both the dying person and those surrounding him with a unique opportunity for spiritual transformation. Over the many years I have been involved with the dying I have observed that those who have allowed the experience of death to enter their hearts have had a profound spiritual awakening. In their last weeks or days these people seem to experience a 'transcension' of self, and a heightened awareness of love. They may die, but they are healed.

This experience seems remarkably akin to the Near Death Experiences now vividly documented and medically accepted.[19] On its deepest levels there is almost a complete renewal of consciousness. A continued and profound insight into death seems to produce a microcosm of the entire spiritual path. At this level a healing death becomes both a spiritual practice and a theology.

To the degree that we are open to receive this transmission, the heart of the healer is awakened to true compassion. It is in this context that love alone acts, in a dialogue where "self" and "other" disappear. The moments when this occurs engage the most profound of human emotions, for they represent on a literal level the drowning of self in the ocean of love. The experience of death, in all its poverty, pain, and helplessness, may simultaneously be the experience of "pure witnessing" in all its glory, majesty and abundance. When we are awakened to love at this level, we experience not only our own pain but that of all humanity as well. When our heart beats in rhythm with the heart of all humanity, we actualize the inseparability of love and healing. It is this love which has for its base the death of self that leads at its deepest level to God.

# Notes:

1  Shakespeare, *King Lear,* (Princeton University Press, 1945.) Act II, scene ii.
2  Philipe Aries, *The Hour of Our Death,* (Vintage Books, New York, 1982) p. 587.
3  Geoffrey Gorer, *Death, Grief and Mourning,* (Anchor Books, New York, 1949) p. 35-37.
4  Philipe Aries, *The Hour of Our Death,* p. 589.

5 Elizabeth Kubler-Ross, *On Death And Dying,* (Macmillan, New York, 1969).

6 Philipe Aries, *The Hour of Our Death,* p. 590.

7 Stephen Levine, *Who Dies,* (Anchor Books, New York, 1982).

8 Stanislav and Christina Grof, *Beyond Death,* (Thames and Hudson, London, 1980).

9 Northrop Frye, *The Top of the Tower,* (McGraw Hill, New York, 1979) p. 100.

10 Marcea Eliade, *The Myth of the Eternal Return,* (Princeton University Press, 1971) p. 162.

11 Rumi, *The Mathnawi of Jaualu'adin Rumi,* (Gibb Memorial Series, London, 1926-1943) p. II 1940.

12 Stanislav and Christina Grof, *Beyond Death,* p. 11-17.

13 Michael Harner, *The Way of the Shaman,* (Bantam Books, New York, 1980).

14 Guenon, Apercus Sur Initiation, (See *Treasury of Traditional Wisdom,* Edited by Whitehall Perry, p. 205).

15 Angelus Silesius, Cherub I 30 (See *Treasury of Traditional Wisdom,* p. 204).

16 ibid.

17 ibid.

18 Plotinus, *The Enneads* as translated by Stephen MacKenna Faber and Faber, London 1956) p. I. vi. p. 6.

19 See Kenneth Ring's *Life At Death* (Coward, McCam and Geohegan, New York, 1980). Also see Raymond Moody's *Life After Life* (Bantam Books, New York).

# "I Am," the Healer

## by Frances Horn

What is true healing? And what is the place of the healer within the healing process? In my eighty years, I seem to have experimented with a whole range of answers to these vital questions. Through the process of "discovering the healer," with its leaps of understanding and moments of self-discovery, I have experienced the vital importance of a surrendered heart. When our primary motivation is to be totally available to the life process, any distinction between "healer" and "healee" dis- appears, and there is only one I AM.

As an adventurous little girl, I was forever skinning my knees. I even remember one escapade when I tried lying flat on my stomach on a swing. Having got up a pretty good speed, I unexpectedly shot off head first, face down, and emerged with skinned forehead, nose, both cheeks, and both knees. In those early days it was always my mother (fortunately a trained nurse) who acted as the healer.

Over the years I managed to experience an assortment of fractures, infections, and surgeries for which the healer was always a medical doctor. At the university I majored in pre-medical training, and had visions of being an eminent surgeon. What saved me (and the world) from that fate was that I had an

Frances Horn, Ph.D. is an 80-year-old native of the San Francisco Bay Area, California. She earned her B.A. from the Univ. of California in 1929 and, at the age of 73, her Ph.D. in counseling psychology from the University for Humanistic Studies. Her most recent 'post-retirement' work is in psychotherapy with cancer patients. Her earlier practice included counseling around adoptions, group therapy, and treatment programs for hospitalized alcoholics and schizophrenics. She is presently active as a writer and lecturer in the U.S., Europe, Australia, New Zealand and South Africa. She is the author of the acclaimed autobiography I Want One Thing. (see pg. 240) appalling fear of mathematics, and knew that I could never pass the remaining pre-medical course, which was college physics. So I switched to psychology.

In later years when I was facing painful personal problems, I underwent psychoanalysis with a Freudian analyst, who thus became the healer. As I look back I conclude that whatever measure of healing occurred during that period came from the experience that another human being could still accept me, even after knowing everything about me!

Through an illness of my husband, we began to study "New Thought." Spiritual mind treatment was used in varying forms, to demonstrate changes in circumstances. Parking places and money were reported as having been found when needed; so too were freedom from such emotions as anger, resentment, fear, and freedom from physical diseases including cancer. The healer was called a practitioner, and the profundity of his or her spiritual understanding varied greatly, and affected the healing experience in both "healer" and "healee."

Meanwhile, the psychologists in America were making changes in their professional organizations, to reflect the expan-sion of consciousness of some of their members. First there was the American Psychological Association. Then a group formed itself as the Association for Humanistic Psychology. Still later, there came to be the Association for Transpersonal Psychology. Out of this, with a wider view, emerged the International Transpersonal Association.

Dr. Frances Vaughan, a clinical psychologist and former president of the Association for Transpersonal Psychology, has written penetratingly of the uniqueness of psychotherapy in a transpersonal context. "From a transpersonal viewpoint, every client is seen as having the capacity for self-healing. The therapist does not cure an ailment for a client, but enables a client to tap inner resources and allow the natural healing or growth process to occur. Beyond this is the possibility of self-transcendence and transpersonal realization, in which the separate and isolated ego may be seen as illusory, while the underlying oneness of existence is experienced as real. The therapist's assumption is that, given the opportunity, the inner wisdom of the organism will emerge as an integrating healing force that the client can trust." [1]

Through the meetings and publications of the Association for Transpersonal Psychology,[2] and through personal contacts with leaders like Frances Vaughan, Roger Walsh, and many others, I began to feel that in psychology itself there was a space that could embrace my own deepest spiritual understanding. As I noted in my autobiography, *I Want One Thing*,[3] as the years passed, I gained understanding of what we really *are*, and was finding a way of living beyond self-possession, in a realm of joyful identification with a universal creative process which expresses itself in our actions, and is equally available in every moment.

Originally, this was based for me on a critical, historical study I had done in my early 20's on the records of the life of Jesus, in the three books we call Matthew, Mark, and Luke. It had been clear to me that what was required of human beings was to surrender the separate, personal will, and to allow one's life to be lived by a "life," a "wholeness," a "creative process" of which one was a part. Little by little I grew in seeing what this meant, and what it asked of me.

I found myself in Australia at this time, attending a con-ference of the International Transpersonal Association, along with many I knew, and many whom I was meeting for the first time. Among the latter was Dr. Paul Blythe, a Canadian psych-ologist who was living and working in Australia. I attended his workshop, and he and his wife Libby attended mine, which happened to be about the work I was doing with patients with cancer. In the wondrous way that such things can happen, we *recognized* one another, felt a deep bond, and knew that our lives had the same spiritual foundation.

They told me about Emissary Foundation International and got me in touch with a San Francisco psychotherapist named Rod Shorter. Since *I Want One Thing* was about to be published, I introduced myself to Rod by sending him a copy, and from that point, all heaven broke loose! I found myself discovering again the core of the teaching of Jesus I had first touched at age 21. The inspiration I experience when I hear or read Emissary teachings, or spend time with those who live the principles, is always intensified as they echo teachings like: "Lose your life to find it" [4] or " do the will of God and not your own will."[5] For example:

"Human bodies, minds and hearts...have been stolen from the Source and used for their own purposes... There is one truth, there is one Source, there is one God, there is one Whole, and we can't have our separate little purposes, either as individuals or states, without regard to the natural order of the whole. There is no existence outside of the whole..."[6]

"Let the design emerge because we identify with the strong and stable current of life, which is the spirit of God..."[7]

"...expression through attunement with the creative process."[8]

And that's where the heart of the healer should be: In a state of total availability to express the purposes of life, the source, the creative process. Such a healer has awakened, at least in some degree, to the illusory nature of usual human experience. Recognizing one "wholeness" that is being everyone and every - thing, the healer sees divinity in the person seeking help. This means that what is in the heart of the healer is love for a fellow-being who *is God,* no matter how contradictory the appearance may seem to be. And the feeling that radiates from the heart of such a healer is love – unconditional love.

The healer is totally available to act in whatever way fits each situation, moment by moment. The intention is not to change a particular condition or to bring about a specific, preconceived good. The intention, from a surrendered heart and mind is to "let love radiate, without concern for results."[9] The renunciation of concern for specific outcomes is possible because of trust in the limitless, mysterious, creative process itself. This creative process is at work in – is already *being* – the one who comes for help. Thus, in the most profound sense, "All is well." The task is to allow this state to express, in one's self, without obstruc - tion from egotisic distortions.

I can offer you a small example from my own life. The case of Gertrude Karnow, also a psychotherapist, represents an experience in which another person and I learned a great deal about what the creative process can achieve through a surrendered heart.

She was found to have a lump in her breast. In the course of our mutual self-discovery, I found I could not be totally avail - able to Life as long as I was wanting her not to want to die, and wanting her to have a biopsy and surgery. Preconceived notions on my part of what should happen were an obstacle to the free movement of the life current. A healer whose intention is to have a heart totally available to the creative process can help a patient renew contact with that Source, that Wholeness. The task for me as a therapist was to accept her exactly as she was, and to see the reality of Being, namely, God being Gertrude.

For those facing the possibility of a life-threatening disease in one's body, there is great value in digging deep into one's self to answer the question, "Is it possible that some part of me could want to die?" Honest answers can reveal a previously unrecognized desire for deep change in one's life. If one sees no way to make such changes, death may unconsciously be offering the desired change. Gertrude's openness to her own spirituality helped her to take certain inner steps, yet long-standing rigidities in the way she regarded surgical procedures made her refuse other possibilities. She had a measure of trust in her intuitive knowing, yet remained blind to the presence of long-held beliefs that were blocking her path.

Four months after discovering the lump, she eventually gave whole-hearted agreement to a biopsy, and to surgery, and she sailed through them in a marvelously heightened level of consciousness. Later she said that what had been determinative for her in our work together was my acceptance of her right to make this life or death choice, herself, from the deepest level of her being. She said, "If someone can have that faith in your being, in your process – that's unconditional love. That leaves you wholly free."

This was ten years ago, and Gertrude Karnow's life continues to express what she *is,* which means 'what *God is* as Gertrude.' She has given herself to whatever means she finds to deepen, clarify and purify her expression. In her work as a therapist, with individuals and with groups, she radiates healing love.

So what is true healing? My present definition, which continues to grow daily, is that there is healing when there is true attunement with the life process. There is healing when the illusion of our being a separate self, vulnerable and self-centered, is replaced by surrender to, communion with, identi -

fication with the limitless Whole of which everyone and everything is part.

What about the healing of the body? What about the healing of emotions, mind, relationships, outer circumstances? I have to tell you that as of now, these seem to me to be secondary. If my primary motivation is to express, freely and fully, whatever the creative process is being as me, then I must tread lightly on the territory that says, "I don't like this pain. I want to be rid of this disease. I can't stand that person. I don't want to die."

In the place of all of this, I can rest quietly at what feels like a changeless center. Deeply, I feel at peace, at home, free. The love that radiates from this place may or may not contribute to the change of a particular condition. But if the universe is what it seems, then such radiation may be all that is required: universal love in expression.

## Notes:

1   Roger N. Walsh, M.D., Ph.D. and Frances Vaughan, Ph.D. (Eds.), *Beyond Ego: Transpersonal Dimensions in Psychology,* J.P. Tarcher, Los Angeles, 1980, pp. 182-183.

2   The Association for Transpersonal Psychology, P.O. Box 3049, Stanford, CA 94305

3   Frances Horn, *I Want One Thing,* DeVorss & Co., Marina Del Rey, 1981.

4   *Luke* 17:33

5   *Luke* 22:42

6   Excerpt from a talk given by Lord Exeter, transcribed and made available by Emissary Educational Services, Loveland, Colorado.

7   ibid.

8   Excerpt from a talk given by Michael Burghley, Emissary Educational Services, Loveland, Colorado.

9   ibid.

# Love Therapy:
# A Soviet Insight

## by Victor Krivorotov

> And he touched her hand, and the
> fever left her: and she arose, and
> ministered unto them.
> *(Matthew 8:15, King James V.)*

If one observes one's unconscious movements, it is not difficult to note that when we develop a pain, the first thing we do is to put a hand on the painful spot; and often, in simple cases, the pain is relieved. Every mother does the same thing when a child complains of not feeling well. It seems evident that this fact was observed in ancient times and made use of in succoring the sick. In accordance with modern usage in the Soviet Union, we have arbitrarily designated this method of treatment as "bioenergotherapy." Such therapy has a history that is thousands of years old. Many centuries before the Christian era, it was used in ancient India. This is borne out by the *Vedas,* a literary monument created in the late 2nd and early 1st millennia B.C.

The priests of ancient Egypt mention this kind of treatment in papyri that have come down to us. In the age of Rameses (late

*Victor Alexeievich Krivorotov, Ph.D. is a remarkable Russian eclectic: psychologist, sportsman, painter and Russian Orthodox mystic. A former champion at rowing and volleyball, he now serves as sports psychologist of a national Soviet tennis team. Victor's father, a former Red Army colonel, was famous throughout the Soviet Union as a 'psychic healer,' a phenomenon studied much more seriously in the U.S.S.R. than in the West. Drawing on all these experiences, Victor has developed a method for treating psychological disorders. Groups using the 'Krivorotov method' of group therapy are active in several Soviet cities and in the U.S.A. He lives with his wife, Louise, and their two children in Tbilisi, Georgian Soviet Socialist Republic.*

12th and early 11th centuries B.C.) the healer Totembi is said to have treated patients by the laying on of hands. His name means: "Lord by his own will and master of his own fingers."

The ancient Greek ruler Solon (6th century B.C.), who is famous for his reforms, wrote: "If hands are laid on a person very painfully afflicted by evil and a grave illness, he promptly recovers."

Pyrrhus (4th century B.C.), the king of Epirus, was a master of the art of healing by the laying on of hands.

The Roman writer Pliny the Elder (1st century B.C.) wrote: "There are persons whose bodies are endowed with a healing force."

The New Testament makes repeated mention of this kind of healing. And the history of Christianity is replete with the names of saints who cured multitudes by laying on of hands.

From century to century, this kind of treatment was handed down by means of demonstration and tradition. The first attempts at investigating it scientifically were made in the 19th century.

The Viennese doctor Mesmer (1741-1815) devoted great effort to reviving "magnetism," as this kind of treatment was then called.

In 1825 the question of magnetism was taken up by the Paris Academy of Medicine, which formed a committee to monitor the treatment for five years at hospitals and in private practice. After observation and evaluation, magnetism was unanimously approved by the members of the commission as an effective therapeutic method.

The year 1887 saw the founding in France of a special French "Society of Magnetizers," which had a school where instruction in the theory of magnetism was given.

In 1912, at the Thirteenth International Medical Congress, magnetism was recognized as a legitimate method of therapy. At that time it was widely practiced in Russia, Germany, Switzerland, England and other countries.

In the 20th century, magnetism has yielded much ground to rapidly and successfully developing pharmacology, which fully corresponds to the requirements of our age with its powerful rhythm of technological progress.

## The Basis of the Therapeutic Relationship

The basis for the present paper is the practical experience of the Krivorotov family, developed over three generations. The founder of this tradition is Alexei Eremeyevich Krivorotov, whose half-century of experience served as the basis for the development of similar capacities in his sons, grandsons and pupils. His methods are still regarded as an example by those who, without knowing him personally, have followed in his footsteps. The human record also remains, in the form of the thousands of people for whom the touch of Alexei Krivorotov's hands brought not only physical health, but his invisible priceless gift: a love of humankind.

But what is the therapeutic factor in the laying on of hands?

In our age of technological progress, when science is describing for the first time a variety of hitherto unsuspected energies and fields, the thought naturally arises that a certain bio-energy transmitted via the hands effects the cure.

For several decades, my father – at first independently and then along with me and in collaboration with the various scientific institutions – sought experimental evidence of the mysterious bio-energy. The search has not yet revealed a quant - ifiable, empirical therapeutic energy, but it has considerably

deepened our understanding of the nature of interactions be -
tween human beings.[1]

As we have gone deeper into the practice of healing, we have
ever more frequently come across instances of healing *without*
the touch of the hands and even without direct social contact. We
have had to recognize that, while the healer's hands undoubtedly
effect a certain action via energy, physical touch has not been
proven to be the only, or even the primary, method of trans -
mission.

We began to research the possibility of long-range inter -
action between human beings. The most important experiment to

---

[1] "...the Soviet Union has some well-known and respected psychic healers
who, it is claimed, can cure all kinds of illnesses by the laying on of hands.
...Colonel Alexei Krivorotov ...worked for over seven years as a psychic
healer in conjunction with his son.

A patient, having been carefully examined and diagnosed by [Victor]
Krivorotov, is placed in a chair. The colonel stands behind the sick person
holding his hands about five centimeters from the patient's body. Starting
from the head, he works his way down the back. Patients usually report
feeling great heat radiating from the colonel's hands, although his hands do
not touch them...

Soviet scientists test[ed] Krivorotov using the Kirlian photography
method. A month of extensive experiments took place...the high-frequency
photos of Krivorotov's hands as he healed showed a complete change in
energy patterns coming from his skin. 'Before,' 'During,' and 'After' Kirlian
pictures showed distinctive characteristics. The brightness of the emission
and the strength of the flares from his hands depended on whether Krivorotov
was tense or relaxed. At the moment when he seemed to be causing a
sensation of intense heat in a patient, the general overall brightness in
Krivorotov's hands decreased and in one small area of his hands a narrow
focused channel of intense brilliance developed. It was almost as if the
energy pouring from his hands could focus like a laser beam.

The Kirlian technique also showed variations in the pain the patients
were experiencing; bright, intense colors for strong pain; pastel colors as
pain diminished." [From *Psychic Discoveries Behind the Iron Curtain*,
Bantam, New York, 1971, p. 222-223 - ed.]

study in that area of our research was performed in 1983-84. It was designed to measure telepathic interaction between two groups of people separated by the maximum distance on Earth's surface. One of the groups, the American, was formed at the Esalen Institute in San Francisco, and consisted of 12-15 persons headed by Mary Payne and Joan Steffie. The other, the Soviet group, comprised a like number of persons and was formed in Tbilisi, drawn from the psychological training group led by Victor Krivorotov, Louise Krivorotova, and Emily Vartanova. The series of experiments was successful, and on the basis of that investigation we concluded that telepathic function is one of the basic psychological functions of humankind. By means of telepathic connection, it seems likely that all people are in close and permanent interaction, which makes it possible to consider humankind as a single organism, preserving its exis - tence and maintaining its organic identity through this function.

In this light, the therapeutic interaction between two persons is revealed as a very complex process which undoubtedly em - braces all strata of the nature of a human being. With such an approach, it becomes necessary to deepen our investigation of the human being in order to discover the mechanisms at work in the therapeutic relationship.

The psychological nature of a human being is effectively and thoroughly revealed in the process of group psychological train - ing. Many years of research in that area of psychology have radically changed our notion of the nature of therapeutic inter - action between human beings. In order to better understand the process, however, we must first ask the question: "What is disease?"

*Victor Krivorotov*

# What is Disease?

This question is undoubtedly very complex. In order to answer it we must sharply define such key concepts as the soul, spirit and love.

It should be noted that a human being is a very complex system of interacting subsystems. Therefore, if we are dealing with the health of the body, we must also deal with the health of the other subsystems at that level of differentiation.

Today, no one doubts that our body is structured as a system. Therefore, if a patient consults a doctor about a pain in his liver, the doctor will necessarily also examine his stomach, kidneys, heart, and so forth.

In the same way, such subsystems of a human being as the body, the soul, and the spirit are systematically correlated.

In addressing the question of health, the systemic principle of the collective structure of all human beings on the social level is also important.

Modern science has already begun to approach an under - standing of the human being as a system, containing the basic levels of spirit, soul and body. That branch of knowledge known as "psychophysiology" has already accumulated a great amount of factual material, and entire areas of new therapy have been created. But the simplified differentiation of a human being into the psyche and the soma does not sufficiently reveal the basic patterns of our systemic nature.

What are the basic components of the body-soul-spirit system, and how are they correlated?

## The Soul

By "soul" is meant, in this paper, the system of psycho - logical traits of a characterological nature which, to a consider - able degree, regulate the behavior of a human being. This system includes principles, character traits, habits, complexes, phobias, psychological states, etc.

The study of the body-soul-spirit system may be extended by more deeply considering each of its elements. Thus the following are components of the soul: the system of values, the world-view, the energy system, and the system of conditioned responses.

a) The work of all the other subsystems depends on the system of values. If it is deficient, a person begins to make mistakes on all other levels, which eventually leads to an interruption of normal function on the physiological level. A system of values which results in a person's being in harmony on all levels of life activity may be said to be free of deficiencies.

b) A false world-view engenders a deficient system of values, which leads to disease.

Practically speaking, the majority of people regard the world around them as an object from which one must procure pleasure. In such a case, the purpose of life is to raise the number and variety of pleasures to a maximum.

A person taking this approach, by exploiting his physio - logical functions to the full, brings them into a pathological state, thereby paying with his health.

A person taking this approach becomes the enemy of others, since he wants to have more than others; in order to get more, he must take it from those around him.

This world-view leads to the deformity of all systems. As a result, he who takes more than all others is left with nothing, and he who gives all, receives all.

This truth is the simplest, the oldest, and the most difficult to actualize if a person has not grasped the systemic nature of his existence on all levels.

c) The energy system comprises such states as cheerfulness, joy, peacefulness, anger, dejection, melancholy, depression, fear, etc.

Cheerfulness and joy are states in which active energy is channeled toward a constructive aim. Peacefulness is the optimum state of open energetics. In this state the highest psychic functions of a person are intensified.

Anger is a state of active, outwardly-directed (open) energy negatively oriented.

Depression, melancholy, and fear are states of closed (inwardly-directed) energy. If a person remains in one of these states for a long time, all somatic systems go into an energetic crisis. These phenomena are now being very actively researched by scientists specializing in the field of psychosomatics.

The organs of the body which are frequently active, in particular the digestive and cardiovascular systems, are the first to be affected by an energetic crisis. The rhythm of modern life necessitates intensive work by the heart. As for the stomach and intestines, most people are constantly digesting food since they eat frequently and the food is complex in nature.

At first glance, anger, as compared to melancholy, presents no danger to a person: the energy structure is outer-directed, and the physical body is stimulated. But if one probes more deeply, one sees that anger sooner or later turns into depression. The destructiveness of anger usually engenders a reciprocal pressure from society, and a general aggravation of the conditions of existence. This often leads to depression, with its accompanying interruptions of normal physical function.

Cheerfulness and joy are excellent states for the soma. But they paralyze the highest psychic functions, without which a person may begin to make mistakes, which in turn leads to dejection. The end result is that the body is again afflicted.

The state of peacefulness, which corresponds to the har - mony of all systems and implies complete health, is attainable only by establishing order in all the subsystems of the human being and, above all, in the system of values and world-view.

Thus the energy system is closely tied in with all the other subsystems. If it remains in one state for a long time, there is a restructuring in the system of conditioning, the system of values, the world-view, the spirit, and finally the body. Conversely, changes in any of the subsystems affect the state of the energy system.

d) Finally, the most important component of the soul in a practical sense is the system of conditioned responses, which to a considerable degree determines the nature of a person's life activity. This system includes character traits, habits, complexes, phobias, etc.; i.e., those programs that strictly regulate a person's behavior.

The most serious afflictions of the system of conditioning are such character traits as egotism, arrogance, vanity, and so on. They affect the corresponding system of values and world-view, and through those subsystems cause dissension and hostility among people, which again leads to somatic disruption. On the other hand, goodness, generosity, love, and tolerance link one person to another into a single whole, which makes for harmony on all levels and absolute health.

All of the components of the soul are correlated not only with one another, but also with the body and, naturally, the spirit. This differentiated picture of our systemic nature may be even further extended by examining the Spirit.

## The Spirit

A person's spirit is that highest principle which determines the unity of one person with another, and of each individual with the universal Spirit.

The basis for the formation of the spirit is a soul which is oriented by its system of values and the world-view toward unity and harmony.

The purpose of a person's life consists in the full actual - ization of the potential inherent in the spirit.

An awakened spirit is the perfect healer of the soul, the system of values, the world-view and, of course, the body.

Spiritlessness – i.e., an orientation toward pleasure rather than understanding and harmony, toward egocentricism rather than love and forgiveness – dooms a person to disease and a meaningless existence. No medication can arrest the deterior - ation of a body which has lost its spiritual connection. We no sooner approach the cure of cancer, than we are threatened by AIDS. If and when we overcome this latest threat, new diseases will appear. But even if medicine succeeds in preserving an individual body that has severed itself from its spiritual connection, we cannot escape the larger effects of this kind of function in the social body, i.e. catastrophes, natural disasters, wars, ecological problems, etc.

Further evidence for the systemic principle is found in the social nature of man. Each person is an important element in the systemic unity of all human beings, which means that individual life activity is closely tied to the life activity of the surrounding whole. The systemic nature of social life means that the quality of the existence of an individual depends on the quality of the interaction among all people. Accordingly, there are individual diseases which are essentially social, because they can be cured only by means of social therapy. Social diseases include elemental disasters, epidemics, catastrophes, and other events deforming the lives of large numbers of people.

A person cannot be in a state of well-being if those around him are experiencing suffering.

Spirituality is the only means of defense against social diseases, since it preserves the universal unity. A spiritual person realizes his relatedness to the condition of those around him.

Thus all the systems and subsystems of human nature at all levels are interdependent. A deformity in any system affects all the rest. Modern man for the most part recognizes only deformations on the somatic level, resulting in a medical structure oriented only toward curing diseases of the body. Much modern psychology is also ineffective at treating behavioral disorders, as it lacks the concepts of the soul and the spirit. To see the whole picture it is essential to take cognizance of the way disease affects all the systems, and to diagnose the disease in that system which is the source and start treatment there.

A modern doctor has no doubt that it is senseless to treat a headache if it is due to an ailing stomach. Similarly, it is sense - less to treat only the body if the cause of its disease lies in arro - gance for example, i.e. in the soul. The physical body tends to absorb the effects of ill function in the system as a whole in or - der to maintain equilibrium. Thus, somatic diseases are a means of protecting the system as a whole against disease. By trying to restore only bodily functions, we often upset the balance of the whole system, which in its turns leads to even greater systemic pathologies. Hence, quite often in trying to cure the body, we damage the system as a whole.

This excursion into the nature of the human being makes it possible to define disease as follows:

A disease is that state of the system in which full spiritual potential is unrealized.

Deformations inside any one of a person's subsystems are reflected in the state of the other systems and the whole, and lead to a drop in spiritual potential.

Given this definition of disease, what does effective treatment consist of?

Treatment consists in stimulating the patient's spirit, which affects all the systems, bringing them into a harmonious state.

The stimulation of the spirit may be accomplished in one of two ways: either directly or by correcting the subsystem which is the initial source of the disease.

For the most part, modern medicine effects somatic correc-tions. Consequently, treatment can be successful only in those cases where the initial source of the disease is in the body. But for modern man, the primary source of disintegration has become a negative system of conditioning (manifesting egotism, arrogance, vanity, envy, jealously, etc.), the system of values, and the world-view.

The most effective method of treatment involves a resonance between patient and healer, such that the malfunctioning subsystem or all subsystems of the patient begin to function in unison with the corresponding subsystems of the healer, which leads to a cure. The high spiritual potential of the healer can instantly bring all of the patient's subsystems into a harmonious state. This is the highest form of treatment. It is the one described in the New Testament. It does not require any physical contact or direct interaction.

As for curing a patient using the physical hands, it is legitimate only when there has been spiritual stimulation and the prior correction of all the higher subsystems.

From this point of view, the practice of healing by the laying on of hands is simply the end product of the process which is brought into play by the resonant presence of the body of the healer. In this case, the entire spectrum of physical energies functioning in a patient's body begins to restructure itself in unison with the corresponding wellness field of the healer, and our search for some healing 'bio-energy' loses its meaning in a larger understanding.

Naturally, the healer oriented toward somatic resonance must himself be physically healthy. As for spiritual stimulation, it is effected without somatic resonance.

In what way does the healer enter into resonance interaction with the patient?

The technique of such contact is called 'love.' Love is the highest form of interaction – one in which the loving person is fully dissolved in the the object of love, giving himself entirely. This is the absolute sacrifice of the self; absolute unity; the maximum actualization of the spirit, to which nothing physical – distance in particular – is an obstacle.

Such being the case, any person capable of spiritual love can be a healer. But if our priority is to live in luxury, seeking pleasures, and addicted to material values, at a time when a third of the earth's population is undernourished and dozens of children starve every hour; if we are afflicted with egotism, pride, and vanity; if we are strangers to tolerance, generosity, and empathy; if we are far removed from the idea of universal unity, then our spirit is paralyzed. We are then incapable of loving and hence cannot be healers.

The role of healer may be played not only by an individual, but by a group of people united by love. The group healer can heal not only individual diseases, but also social ones. This mission has historically been carried out by communities of monks. Unfortunately, they are becoming fewer and fewer today.

The church has always played the role of a social healer, but its influence has been weakened owing to scientific progress. But scientific progress has not yet created its own methods of social healing, despite the existence of high technology.

Today, socio-psychological training has become very promising. If it is skillfully oriented toward the actualization of the spirit, it can serve to effect the most radical changes on the level of all of humanity's subsystems. An element of social healing can be detected in modern communications, which link people daily in dozens of ways. If these connections are used properly, they can assist social healing to a high degree.

Thus, the chief conclusion of our investigation is that *love is the prime therapeutic factor in any real healing.* Any other therapy can do no more than point the way to love.

The highest form of love at the individual level of social healing is love for one's enemy: the principle of turning the other cheek. Very often, this principle is misunderstood. All human beings, collectively, are a whole organism, and there are no enemies among us. Our real 'enemy' is the anger that is stirred up in our heart when we are contradicted in one way or another. In this sense, to love one's enemy means to preserve our spirituality, and to preserve a state of love within our selves; i.e., to preserve oneself in a situation that might seem to demand losing oneself in the mire of anger and aggression. To love one's enemy means to turn our face from any aggression within us. Essentially, love for one's enemy is the highest form of struggle against oneself; i.e., the internal enemy, since there are no external enemies. If we think in practical, realistic terms, turning the left cheek when we have been hit on the right is the most perfect method of stopping the striking hand.

The logical Christian has never had any external enemies. He has only one enemy: his own passions. One who interprets the "other cheek" principle as servility merely demonstrates the interpreter as a stranger to spiritual understanding. Ever since the inner world was revealed to us, the principles of "an eye for an eye" and "a tooth for a tooth" have not signified a struggle, but a defeat, because "an eye for an eye" is not conquered passion but redoubled passion. In any situation, be it disease, relationships or international wrangles, the only true victory is the triumph of the spirit.

# Healing Prayer

## by Francis MacNutt

In the past few years an extraordinary change has been going on in the Roman Catholic Church — all the way from the grassroots level to the most official pronouncements: the healing ministry is being renewed.

On the part of official pronouncements the most far-reaching of all the changes in understanding the sacraments went into effect January 1, 1974. The "Anointing of the Sick" is now for the professed purpose of healing the whole man and is no longer primarily a preparation of the soul for death. In line with this reorientation of the sacrament's purpose, it is to be administered not just to those in danger of death, but to anyone suffering from a serious illness.[1] These changes represent a return to an earlier view of the Anointing of the Sick prevalent in the Church until the time of the Middle Ages.

At the same time, at the grass-roots level we are seeing prayer groups rediscovering the power of praying for the sick. This is not just a theoretical change; it is a change based on people's experience who have seen the sick healed through prayer. On a typical Pentecostal retreat now when I ask for a show of hands of those who have seen the sick healed through their prayers about half the hands go up. Similarly, when I ask

*Francis MacNutt, Ph.D. was one of the first Catholics to become involved in the 'charismatic renewal' movement. He became well known world-wide for his special gift of healing, which took him to some 33 countries, including India, Australia, Peru, and Poland. A graduate of Harvard University and Aquinas Institute of Theology, Francis is now the director of Christian Healing Ministries, and resides in Jacksonville, Florida with his wife, Judith and their two children. He has authored the bestselling books:* The Power to Heal *and* Healing, *which has been described as "...the most scholorly and comprehensive book on Christian healing...ever." (see pg. 240)*

This chapter is based on material taken from *Healing* by Francis MacNutt (Notre Dame, IN: Ave Maria Press, 1974).

how many think, as far as they can judge, that any of their own illnesses have been healed through prayer, about half the hands go up.

Yet, I can remember a few short years ago when even the Catholic charismatic prayer groups had reservations about praying for physical healing.

My own involvement in the healing ministry came about in a very natural way; I never had much internal resistance to overcome — except lack of courage. My question has never really been as to its reality, but as to its wise use.

I was first prepared for this ministry by my desire to become a doctor, a desire which was nearly fulfilled in 1944 when I was accepted by Washington University Medical School after only two years of college premed. If all had gone well I would have become a doctor at the young age of 23, but that dream was blasted when I was drafted in September of 1944, just ten days before entering med school. The next two years I served in the Medical Department of the Army as a surgical technician, mostly working in the operating room of the hospital at Camp Crowder, Missouri.

Years later, when I entered the Dominican Order and read the lives of the saints with all the fervor of those novitiate days, I couldn't help but wonder why they seemed to have so much success going around healing the sick through their prayers, while we were never encouraged to pray for such things. We got the impression that praying for healing was presumptuous, like pretending to be a saint — which I certainly was not. We were not worthy of extraordinary manifestations of God's power.

How clearly I remember my Protestant friend who came and asked me to heal his son's partial blindness. This was in July, 1956, only a month after my ordination, and I didn't know how to respond to him. One thing I did know was that I was no saint, so I refused to go over to his home. I knew I was disappointing him but I felt I would disappoint him even more if I went to his home and his boy was not healed by my prayer.

Later, when I was teaching homiletics at the Aquinas Institute of Theology and was also trying to counsel many people, I felt that something was missing in my ministry. What kind of spiritual direction could I give to all these people coming for counsel — many of them sent by their psychiatrists? They were depressed — some to the point of attempting suicide; some were alcoholic, some homosexual, some hopelessly confused, feeling worthless and unlovable. They were the "not O.K." people, the "frogs."

Their emotional problems could not be separated from their "spiritual" lives; as human beings they were being dragged down by sadness and guilt. Yet they could not overcome their problems by willpower. Some priests, brothers and sisters were among them — people who had dedicated their lives to Christ, but found that they were not able to live happily in community in spite of all their good will. I could not honestly say to myself — or to them — that all this destructive suffering was redemptive. I could not sincerely tell the mentally depressed patient, who was going through shock therapy, that his anxiety state was God's will and was a cross specially chosen by God for him.

Through discussion with Protestant friends who not only believed in praying for healing, but had seen healing take place, I finally took the plunge and attended a School of Pastoral Care in Whitinsville, Maine, in 1968. These seminars were started by Agnes Sanford, a pioneer in the movement of Christian healing, and were for the purpose of teaching ministers and physicians, with their spouses, what Agnes and others had learned through years of study and experience. For me it was a turning point; I was then in my 40's and head of an organization dedicated to improving preaching in the Roman Catholic Church. But I was realizing that the real problem with our preaching was that it was not always acccompanied by God's power to change people's lives and make God's "kingdom come on earth as it is in heaven."

When I discovered, then, that healing was common in the lives of people like Agnes Sanford, it all seemed to make sense: if it were true, it meant I would no longer have to tell people whose sicknesses were disintegrating their personalities that their illness was a God-sent cross. I could hold up the hope that God wanted them well, even when medical science could not help.

The first person I prayed for was a sister who had been through shock treatment for mental depression and had been taken as far as psychiatry could take her. I knew she had nothing to lose by my praying with her. And I had nothing to lose, except a certain false humility, by offering to pray for her healing. To my surprise (at least partly) she was healed. This encouraged me to believe that if *I* prayed for people they might be healed. (Somehow it was much easier to believe that God could could heal the sick *through prayer* than to believe that he would heal *through my prayer*.)

Since then I have seen many people healed – especially when I have prayed with a team or in a loving community. Although I travel too much to be able to follow up and estimate accurately, I would make a rough estimate that about half those that we pray for are healed (or are notably improved) of physical sickness and about three-fourths of those we pray for are healed of emotional or spiritual problems.

In the past eighteen years I think I can safely say that I have seen thousands of healings take place through prayer. Many of these healings taken individually are ambiguous as proof; they can be explained in a variety of ways. Who can say that we know all the factors of a case, so that we can say with certainty, "This remission of disease took place following prayer and therefore prayer caused the healing take place?" But I do believe that anyone who would come with me on retreat after retreat would see so many blessed by healings that he would see a cumulative body of evidence all pointing in the direction of an extraordinary power being present, of a number of healings taking place well beyond the realm of chance occurrence.

Books have been written that document cases of healing and, in an effort to scientifically demonstrate the power of prayer, some fascinating studies have been done on the effects of prayer upon plant growth — something that can be measured and calculated before and after prayer. Rev. Franklin Loehr, for instance, a chemist, reports in his book, *The Power of Prayer on Plants,*[2] the results of 156 persons praying in 700 unit experiments using more than 27,000 seeds and seedlings involving about 10,000 measurements and achieving up to a 52.71 percent growth advantage for prayer seedlings. Other experiments scientifically controlled include "Some Biological Effects of the 'Laying On of Hands,'" by Dr. Bernard Grad,[3] in which he tested the speed with which wounds heal in mice, as well as a remarkable experiment in which the rate of growth of plants was measured when the plants (in this case, rye grass) were prayed for at a distance of 600 miles.[4]

While some of the experiments have an element of the bizarre - testing mice and rye grass - yet these were the most apt scientific controls and were perhaps necessary for a contemporary mentality seeking proof through scientific measurement. It would be a pity if scientists discovered persuasive evidence for the power of prayer at a very time when theologians were calling into question the value of the ancient Christian tradition of praying for the sick. A study of healing in the church had this to say:

"But the average, orthodox clergyman is not much interested in practices that would convey healing. The 'orthodox' Christian, whether liberal or conservative, has little exposure to such sacramental acts and little or no interest in physical or mental healing through religious means. This fact has been brought home to me graphically on several occasions. One was the experience just a few years ago of a friend who is State Commissioner of Health for one of the large eastern states. At this instance a group of doctors and clergy were called together to discuss the whole subject of spiritual healing. While the physicians as a whole were deeply involved in the discussion, the clergy who attended hardly treated the subject as a serious one.

"At about the same time a similar meeting was called by a large western hospital which has a department of religion and health. A selected group of clergy and medical men were invited to meet together and discuss the problems. All but one of the physicians responded and 80 percent of them came, while barely 50 percent of the clergy even answered the letter and less than 30 percent of them attended the meeting."[5]

I personally found most Christians (priests, in particular) very open to discussing the possibility of praying for healing and many have themselves been encouraged to launch out and begin praying for the sick with more confidence than before. They, in turn, bring back encouraging accounts of the visible renewing of their own ministry. A study authorized by the U.S. Roman Catholic bishops in the 1970's went so far as to say:

"Priests today are discovering the power of intercessory prayer as part of their professional practice and spiritual counseling. This prayer is directed at physical and especially inner healing. Serious problems such as drug addiction, alcoholism, and long-seated emotional disturbances in some cases seem to have been helped by priests who recognize the appropriateness of joining prayer to the equally necessary professional counseling. They have seen the power of Christ come through them as channels of His love. As yet not many priests have experienced this power, but for those who have, the problem of discovering the relevance of their ministry has disappeared."6

Such a statement would have been inconceivable just five years before, when I was the first Roman Catholic priest to attend Agnes Sanford's School of Pastoral Care.

In 1980 I married Judith Sewell, a counselor by profession, who had discovered in her own work the need to pray that her clients be cured, rather than just encouraged to cope with their problems for the rest of their lives. Since then we have spoken to many groups and prayed with many more people. We are now involved in establishing a healing center with the active support of the Episcopal Diocese of Florida. As I write this, it is only a week since we had our first conference here in Jacksonville, and the written evaluations indicate that about 90% of the participants experienced healing, at least in some measure. As one woman described her experience:

"I came to the conference hoping to learn more about 'inner healing' since our church is interested in learning about it; but I never expected really to receive healing myself!

"The Lord really touched me on Wednesday night in a very powerful, personal way. Before I stood up to receive prayer, I sensed God's presence in a powerful way. I felt as if I was unable to move out of my chair. I felt an overwhelming peace and stillness throughout my whole being. I was literally being bathed in a golden rain or light – I can't describe it; it was like gold. For a while I felt as if I was literally lifted up into another realm; I really sensed that I was in God's presence briefly. I thought that my self-image had been fairly well healed, but the Lord did some additional healing that evening. It was a beautiful, glorious time in the Lord and one that I will remember all my life. I've been a Christian for a long time but it has been a long time since I've seen God's power manifested as it was that evening."

To me it is heartening to know that many people are now being filled with God's love, joy and peace, and receiving physical healings as well in ways that I once thought were rare and extraordinary!

One thing that we have learned over the years is that most physical healing takes time. I have often had to pray many times, for instance, with an arthritis patient, before the healing seems complete. Often I have had to pray for hours, days or months with a little improvement taking place each time.

As I now see it, prayer is like radiation treatment: the longer the 'cancer' is held within the range of God's healing power, usually conveyed through the laying on of hands, the more the sickness withers up and dies.

The following excerpt from a letter is typical in its simple description of a gradual – but remarkable – process of healing:

"You laid hands on and prayed for my mothers' hip, which used to stick out so much that she could actually rest her arm on it. Since that evening it has continued to go down and into place until now it it even with the other hip. Also, the knots in her back (as a result of the out-of-place hip) have unknotted! Her hip has been like that since she was in a bicycle accident in her 20's. She said to tell you that for the first time in 50 years her skirts fit her."

In no way do I conceive prayer for healing as a negation of the need for doctors, nurses, counselors, psychiatrists or pharmacists. God works in all these ways to heal the sick; the ideal is a team effort to get the sick well through every possible means.

Nevertheless, although I am aware that some prayer can have a psychological effect through the power of suggestion, I am convinced that prayer for healing brings into play forces far beyond what our own unaided humanity contributes. The results of prayer have been extraordinary – so much so that what once would have astonished our retreat team we now take almost for granted. The extraordinary has become ordinary.

And that's the way I think the healing ministry should be: an ordinary, normal part of the life of every community.

*Francis MacNutt*

**Notes:**
1 Study Text II: *Anointing and Pastoral Care of the Sick*
Publications Office, Washington, D.C, U.S. Catholic
Conference, 1973.
2 *Signet,* New York, 1969, reprinted from the 1959 edition.
3 From *The Journal of Pastoral Counselling,* Vol. VI, No.2,
pp.38-41.
4 Op. cit., Robert Miller, *The Effect of Thought Upon the
Growth Rate of Remotely Located Plants,* p. 62
5 Morton T. Kelsey, *Healing and Christianity,* Harper &
Row, New York, 1973, pp. 5-6.
6 ed. Rev. Ernest Larkin, O. Carm., Rev. Gerald Broccolo,
et al, *The Spiritual Renewal of the American Priesthood,*
U.S. Catholic Conference, 1973, Washington, D.C., p 18.

# Passion, Compassion & Medical Practice

## by Ernesto Contreras

For many centuries the practice of medicine was aimed at taking care of the whole individual. It was characterized by com - passion, sympathy, and love toward the sufferer. But in this century, that practice has gradually been transformed into an impersonal, cold, scientific discipline in which the patient has little voice, and is expected to submit unquestioningly to the doctor's authority. This unfortunate change has been the result of assigning too much importance to scientific knowledge and experimental methods which consider the human body purely as a complex machine that has to be repaired by means of advanced technology.

From the start of this century, science virtually declared war on the employment in medicine of spiritual laws and values. Left brain came to dominate right brain; cold knowledge pushed out compassion and love. When the brilliant French astronomer La Place, who published *Celestial Mechanics* in 1799, was asked by Napoleon why he did not dedicate a word to the creator of the heavens he had so elegantly described, the scientist answered: "Sire, my science is not based on hypothesis."

*Ernesto Contreras R., M.D. is a graduate of University of Mexico (B.S. 1932, M.D. 1939). He is the founder, director and medical oncologist of Del Mar Medical Center and Hospital in Tijuana, Mexico (founded 1963). He has been developing cancer prevention programs through the use of metabolic therapy and non-toxic anti-tumor agents since 1965. He is a member of a number of medical associations and author of numerous articles for medical publications. He has a wife, Rita, 6 children and 15 grandchildren and is very active in the Mexican Methodist Church.*

The concept that science has nothing at all to do with God has done much to delay real progress in human knowledge.

The moment a young student begins his studies in medical school, all textbooks and lectures begin the process of brain - washing him into the supremacy of basic science over spiritual values in his future career. When he graduates as a doctor, he is full of the arrogant conviction that he knows a great deal. If he manages to become a specialist, he is molded into into a proud, self-sufficient "professional." He is convinced that with science alone he is capable of solving all the problems of human suf - fering; that to treat a case of typhoid fever, meningitis or cancer he does not need God's assistance. Before the patient he must appear in unquestioning command. He believes it "unprofes - sional" to show emotion, which is equated with weakness. Even doctors who remain committed to spiritual values in their per - sonal lives often start to behave as though they are agnostics the minute they step into the consulting room.

The tender and compassionate heart of the young healer is thus transformed into the cold and insensitive heart of the man of science. This is even more evident in the new generations of oncologists. They are impersonal and removed – even cruel – when the verdict of cancer, with its terrifying future, is handed down to the patient. They even dare to give dates when the patient is expected to die! This attitude has stricken the lives of countless cancer patients, and generally retarded progress in the treatment of cancer.

Our experiences at Centro Medico and Hospital del Mar for the past 23 years lead me to believe that perhaps 25% of cancer patients who die prematurely because of aggressive cancers could live longer, happier lives simply by receiving more per - sonal care, developing better communication with their doctors, and even, perhaps, learning how to love them. How fresh and timely sounds the voice of Ezekiel, the prophet of God, trans -

mitting the gracious promise of his Sovereign Lord to His people: "I will give you a new heart and put a new spirit in you; I will remove from you your heart of stone and give you a heart of flesh."[1]

Any doctor who applies for a full-time position in one of our institutions must be willing to experience this change in his or her heart: we feel the value of a sensitive, compassionate and loving physician cannot be overestimated. We consider it vital that our staff have a practical, living experience of two basic laws:

1 - **The Golden Rule:** Do to your patient as you would do to yourself.

2 - **The Second Commandment:** Love your patient as yourself.

At our institutions we practice medicine with the mind and with the heart; science and art. We use all that science offers, but we know we must use our artistic abilities to make a good diag - nosis, to establish the best treatment, and, of no less importance, to create good rapport with patients and inspire in them confidence, faith, hope and a positive attitude.

To change the heart of stone to a heart of flesh also implies that we have to go back to the healers' underlying assumptions about the nature of the human being. Man is not just a highly evolved animal composed merely of a body and a limited mind. Man is of a different order of creation, with an enormous unex - plored mental capacity and a spirit. He is an indivisible trinity, and whatever affects his body will necessarily disturb his mind and his spirit. For many years doctors, especially in chronic dis - eases, have dedicated all their efforts to treating the physical aspect, artificially leaving aside the other areas. This has been a great mistake that has delayed progress, especially in cancer.

Another negative result of the materialistic practice of medi - cine is the false concept that cancer is initially a local disease that only requires local treatments to be cured, such as surgery and radiation. Cancer, no matter how early it is detected, always will affect the mind and the spirit. In many instances, the real disease starts in those areas and later on will manifest as a physical illness. Thus, cancer should always be considered as a systemic problem in order to establish the proper therapies.

The types of treatment prescribed have also been greatly influenced by the purely scientific and materialistic practice of medicine. In the case of cancer, the degree of aggressiveness the therapies have reached is almost unbelievable – in surgery, the hemicorporectomies and supermasectomies; in radiation therapy, the total body irradiation and massive short term programs; in chemotherapy, the protocols of four or five extremely toxic chemicals. Each of these can produce some good immediate results, but very frequently the price the patient pays as a human being is simply too high. Even in the best hands there is always a risk of death or permanent side effects (iatrongenia), that could result in a very miserable life.

Another basic and long-standing mistake made in con - ventional treatments is that practically all the efforts of the doctor are directed toward destroying or eliminating the malignant cells – a disease-driven model of medicine. And as the aggressive procedures are not selective, they also destroy many healthy cells and damage the patient's immune system. So, when the cancer cells that have survived the initial attack get organized again and produce a relapse, the body is in a very poor condition to fight back.

The programs we have developed, besides being substan - tially less aggressive, give major emphasis to rebuilding the

immune system. This is accomplished by means of detox -
ification, diet, vitamins and other immunostimulants which must
include spiritual therapy and psychotherapy. The more attention
we give to the latter aspects, we have discovered, the better the
chance of effective restoration of the immune system.

This philosophy is not based on hypothetical or purely myst -
ical ideas. It is a realistic approach that is proving to be
extremely helpful. Our patients enjoy a much better quality of
life than under conventional treatment routines, and, frequently,
remarkably long survival periods.

In a recent article a Canadian oncologist[2] expresses the thesis
that serious, ethical doctors must exercise their profession based
on the "biomedical model" which is considered by him to be the
only one which scientifically explains the cause and natural
history of cancer. The "common sense" model is for ignorant
people or quacks.

The facts, however, show that by sticking to this
"biomedical model," oncologists have made little or no progress.
This is the conclusion reached by two reputable professors at the
Harvard School of Public Health. They reviewed thousands of
charts from 1950 through 1982, and, according to that study,
the current cancer treatments should be considered a "qualified
failure." They conclude that "we are losing the war against
cancer," and that more public funds should be devoted to
prevention.[3]

The following three case histories are of very seriously and
terminally ill cancer patients who came to us for treatment. All
are extremely well documented according to orthodox criteria.

**Case 1** – White female, aged 58. In September 1977 she
developed rapid abdominal distension. A sonogram showed a
large mass in the right ovary; laparotomy on September 29. The
surgeon found an advanced, bilateral ovarian adenocarcinoma

with extensive peritoneal implants. In October a strong chemo -
therapy program was started. In March of 1978 it had to be
discontinued because of toxic effects. Then she started metabolic
therapy. In late August of the same year a large recurrent
abdominal mass was removed surgically. She was admitted to
our Institution on September 3, 1979 and was put on a
combination program of metabolic therapy, immunotherapy and
mild chemotherapy.

In January 1981 there was evidence of more tumor growth
in the abdomen causing blockage of the ureters. Her condition
was very critical. On March 25 a right nephrostomy had to be
performed just to make her less uncomfortable. Chemotherapy
was discontinued. In spite of her condition, the patient was
willing to keep fighting and this encouraged us to continue with
the metabolic therapy. By December of the same year she was
doing remarkably well in spite of the fact that the tumor masses
kept growing slowly. In June 1983 she started to show episodes
of partial intestinal obstruction, which gradually got worse and
in May 1984 a transverse colostomy had to be performed.
Prognosis was again very poor, but once more she evidenced
great courage.

Since then, up to February 1987, when she last visited our
hospital as an outpatient, she had been holding up in good
condition, remaining very active, travelling frequently and
seemed very well-adjusted to her ostomies. Her local oncologist
can't explain how she is still living – and happily too! He
encourages her to keep taking the program that has helped so
much. He is convinced that her positive attitude and faith have
been the main factors in her amazing survival.[4]

Case 2 – White female, age 53. For several years she was
exposed to severe emotional stress. During 1981 and 1982 she
suffered frequent spells of diarrhea and cramps which were not

helped by the usual remedies. In early October 1983 she devel - oped acute abdominal pain and noticed that her urine had a fecal odor. She was hospitalized and complete studies showed she had a huge carcinoma of the sigmoid colon. Emergency surgery was performed on October 17 and the surgeon removed the tumor, but he also found involvement of a loop of the terminal ileum which was attached to the urinary bladder forming a fistula, so he had to remove the affected loop and repair the bladder. Her postoperative course was complicated by pulmon - ary edema and myocardial infarction. Radiation therapy and chemotherapy were started in November, but had to be discontinued soon because of intolerance.

On January 9, 1984, she was admitted to our institution in very poor condition and in a terrible state of depression. Given very little chance of survival, we put her on our full program of metabolic therapy, mild chemotherapy (5FU) and a strong program of psychotherapy and spiritual assistance. To our sur - prise, she developed a very positive attitude and started to improve in all aspects. Five weeks later she was discharged in good condition and went home very optimistic. By September of the same year she was doing so well that the mild chemotherapy was discontinued. A CAT scan showed no evidence of tumors in her abdomen. During 1985 and 1986 she enjoyed a very normal life. Her last visit with us was on March 4, 1987. She felt so well that she has asked us to close the colostomy that was done in her first emergency surgery.[5]

**Case 3** – White male, age 53. In September, 1986 he began to suffer from indigestion, excess gas, alarming loss of weight and later, severe pain in his right hip. He was studied and found to have very large liver, a right pulmonary nodule, and a lesion in the lumbar spine. A liver biopsy disclosed a very aggressive metastatic adenocarcinoma and a bone scan detected metastasis

in his fifth lumbar vertebra. The final diagnosis was primary carcinoma of the right lung with massive metastases to the liver and
to the fifth lumbar vertabra. He soon became bedridden with ex-
cruciating pain and started to deteriorate rapidly. Nothing was
offered to him, being so terminally ill.

He was admitted to Hospital del Mar on November 26, 1986
for final care. Medically speaking, he could not live more than 4
to 6 weeks, but the patient and his wife expressed the desire to
fight and the faith that he could still survive longer. Encouraged
by such a positive attitude, we started to treat him. Moderate
doses of radiation therapy were given to the lumbar spine. A
special catheter was inserted in the umbilical vein to administer
Laetrile and some chemotherapy (5FU) directly into the liver.
Nothing was done to the lung.

To our great surprise, the pain subsided completely after the
second week and the patient started to improve in a dramatic
way. By Christmas he was ambulatory. The liver scan showed
definite regression of the metastases and the CEA test went
down. He started to eat well and gain weight. On April 30, 1987
a new liver scan showed 75% regression of the metastases and
the chest x-ray showed no tumor in the right lung.

At the present time the patient is in excellent clinical
condition and we have started to believe that, as incredible as it
might seem, he could go into complete remission.[6]

Scientifically speaking, and applying the concept of the biomedical model so faithfully espoused by the "accepted" medical
establishment, none of these three cases should have survived
long. None of the three received miracle drugs to which we
might attribute the stabilization or remission of their condition.

This indicates to me that the turning points in the course of
their conditions came with the special care and support provided
in the emotional and spiritual areas. Biomedical model doctors

may call these anecdotal cases, spontaneous remissions, cases of the placebo effect, or whatever. What counts is the fact that the three are alive and well at the present time (May 6, 1987).

To ask for a change in the heart of the healer is not a purely hypothetical or mystical request. It is an urgent need if we really want to see more effectiveness in the treatment of chronic degenerative diseases, especially cancer.

Let us pray that in the near future more and more doctors may be willing to humble themselves, accept their limited knowledge, look for divine guidance, and permit their hearts of stone to be transformed into hearts of flesh. Only then may the title "Doctor" become synonymous with that of "Healer."

**Notes:**
1 Ezekiel 36:26
2 M.L. Brigden, M.D. *Postgraduate Medicine,* January 1987, p. 271-280.
3 Bailar III and Smith, *New England Journal of Medicine,* May 8, 1986, 1226-1232
4 Hospital del Mar, Chart CMM-79-17120.
5 Hospital del Mar, Chart CMM-81-20694.
6 Hospital de Mar, Chart CMM-86-27579

# Individual & Collective Transformation

## by Richard Moss, M.D.

It has been over ten years now since I left the practice of traditional medicine in order to answer a call from deep within to learn more about the roots of health and wholeness for myself and all people. It has been ten years since an event of major significance to me occurred and changed the whole course of my life. Not long after that event I wrote an essay entitled: "The Individual and Collective Levels of Consciousness in Health and Disease."

Since that time, I have had a great deal more experience working with people on those issues. Thus, it feels appropriate to undertake an overview of what we call health and the problem of disease.

I must acknowledge that my starting point is a personal experience and therefore a large element of subjectivity enters into the picture that could, for some, diminish the potential scientific and clinical validity of these ideas. This subjective experience stands as a kind of template, a subject beam in the hologram of understanding. Because of this experience, I gained a new understanding of the physical and psychological trans - formation I observed in so many people. Thus the full hologram of understanding gradually emerged as I looked at my own

*Richard Moss, M.D. practiced medicine until 1976, when he initiated his transformational workshops which have since taken him to many countries. He is widely regarded as an inspirational teacher, and facilitator for individuals awakening into new dimensions of consciousness. His work bridges traditional medical, psychological and spiritual thinking. He is the author of* The I That Is We: Awakening to Higher Energies Through Unconditional Love, How Shall I Live: Transforming Surgery or Any Health Crisis Into Greater Aliveness *and* The Black Butterfly: An Invitation to Radical Aliveness. *(see pg. 240)* experience against a series of events involving others. Of these events, the principal ones are the stories of Laura and Theodora, which I have written about in *The Black Butterfly*. In addition, there are many other people who came to me for counseling or participated in conferences and underwent psycho-physical transformation with marked effect upon their health.

Therefore, I feel compelled to review my own experience and the conclusions I have gradually drawn from it. The nature of that experience could be defined using terms from other cultures, such as, "the awakening of kundalini," "conversion," "illumination" and so on. However, these words seem misleading, for they cannot accurately convey what occurred in the period of my late twenties to mid-thirties. Quite abruptly (although there were many contributing factors beforehand), I underwent a fundamental change at a psychophysical level. This was accompanied by – at the physical level – intense autonomic nervous system activation with trembling, anxiety, heart palpitation, weakness, alternating with seemingly limitless strength. I had strange pains that migrated around the body, augmented metabolic functioning, forcing a change in diet habit to frequent small meals, including a craving for meat in small amounts, and a craving for water immersion. In addition, there were changes in vision (on some days, though I have been extremely near-sighted since age 10, I did not require glasses to see), feeling as though my heart were physically breaking, or as though there were a great hole where my chest should be, pain in the spine, frequent muscle fasciculations and spasming, a feeling of drying out, of having the flu but never developing fever or any other symptoms, and many more things.

Of equal, and perhaps greater, importance were the psycho - logical changes that took place. I had a tremendous sense of religious imminence, of being in the presence of the holy of holies. This oscillated with feelings of dread and of dying. I submitted to several medical examinations in order to demonstrate or eliminate the possibility of disease. In general, fear of death and a kind of existential 'angst' was intensified in the immediate period that followed the phases of exalted peace and vastness. I felt a tremendous rapport with people and things – light on leaves, shadows, smells, simple gestures. I was de - lighted in doing simple things such as the dishes. I walked a great deal, feeling as though I was inside of everything around me. Driving down the hill into town was accompanied by a feeling of being crushed, as if the psychic density of people were a palpable substance encroaching on my being and bearing it down with pain. Tears came spontaneously when I read of cruelty and even more so when I read of courage and self-sacrifice for the good of others.

In general, emotion swept through me with a fullness of ex - pression I had never known, yet they passed on so completely and left no residue of psychical content whatsoever. I had the impression (often confirmed) of knowing who was at the door or on the phone, or what someone would say before they said it. What Jung has termed "synchronicity," the intersection of meaning from highly distinct and separate dimensions of reality, was nearly a constant occurrence. My dream life was active and vivid. In addition, I would find myself waking from a dream only to observe the dream continuing even while awake. Fantasies sometimes took on a visible reality, being super - imposed upon ordinary waking consciousness to such a degree that it was like watching a movie with many semi-transparent screens, each showing a different feature. I found this disconcerting at first, but the simple question, "Who are you?" repeated a few times to myself would return me to the 'normal' reality.

Perhaps even more important was the sense of hunger for spiritual literature. I read ferociously of material that had form -

erly been difficult to understand or previously held little meaning for me. There seemed to me a marked increase in a sense of personal authority. That is, there was the sense that "I" existed as a cause unto itself and yet simultaneously this "I" was a part of everything, inseparable from the interior world of conception, fantasy and dream. I had the distinct impression of having been given both a new body and a new consciousness. I would begin to speak and I would find myself expostulating with tremendous insight in areas that I had little exposure to beforehand. I immediately had the capacity to draw upon information stored from memory and to synthesize it, so that new meaning could be derived, and previously disconnected thoughts and feelings were shown to be interconnected and relevant to each other.

People began to tell me that I was putting into words their most remote and hidden intuitions. This ability to bring into the light of awareness what had been previously unavailable was perhaps the most pronounced aspect of the change. A sense of authority made it possible to express these ideas, to create group work so I could delve deeper and finally to write about them in books. My previous self did not feel capable of any real statement of being. I was still locked into my conditioned view of self. This former me had a deep commitment to personal growth, but saw this as work, not fun. The new me felt as though every moment and all action were part of one uninterrupted meditation and prayer.

This is not to say that even now there is never a sense of separation, of falling back, of being a mere beggar before the door of the Infinite. But now I am more able to guide others into a whole new dimension. Yet I am often unable to enter or rest there because I sense there is so much more, and that makes it impossible to remain in any feeling of arrival or completion. It is like a horizon that recedes further and further as we ascend the mountain. Nevertheless, it is safe to say, without any exagger -

ation, that a veil had been lifted away and the universe before me was forever changed and lit with an inner spiritual light and a sense of meaning and wholeness that simply did not exist before. And this experience, while no longer as intense as it was in the newness of that time, nevertheless remains vivid.

In short, I went through a radical transformation of con - sciousness. However, while the psychical aspects were immed - iately obvious to me personally, the possible physical signif - icance did not become apparent until I began to precipitate similar kinds of transformation in others or, at the very least, found myself repeatedly in the position of observing them. At the time of my experience, I was not aware that I had any disease, therefore I was not aware of any miraculous cure in my own body. That I had been miraculously cured of a great deal of fear and psychological limitation was not obvious. I can say that for a while I seemed impervious to illness, despite feeling immensely stressed. But I have since had my share of colds and infection and other problems, so I have no doubt whatsoever of my mortality. If there is any observation about some long term physical differences, it is that since the change I rarely manifest fever though it had been fairly prominent in my colds and flus in the previous years. Also, I find that I can sense most minor illlnesses and can hold them off through the quality of my attention. Thus, I can consciously choose not to be sick, something I do not recall being capable of beforehand.

My own personal experience of transformation leads me to assert that there is a tremendous – and I feel disastrous – tendency in our culture to make a distinction between consciousness and the body. If I were to try to objectify the contribution my work may represent in the area of medicine, it is to *unqualifiedly* lay this error to rest without qualification. It is a distinction that has no basis in fact and which leads us repeatedly into great misunderstanding when we face the mysteries of health and disease. What we call consciousness and the physical expression of the human body are a continuum. If consciousness changes in any degree, there is an equivalent change at the physical level and vice-versa. Yet the challenge is to prove this. And while I did not set out to find such proof – and have not kept detailed clinical records – I have nonetheless come to the irrefutable conclusion that consciousness and the body are inseparable.

Moreover, I have been able to demonstrate this with case histories, and even more importantly, with immediate and direct examples that have been witnessed by hundreds of people, many of whom are physicians. During a conference at my retreat center, I recall one man who was so weakened by his illness that he could hardly walk, yet a few days later he was hiking a steep, difficult trail up a mountain. During conferences, nearly every woman begins menstruating within hours to days of arrival, no matter where in her cycle she has been. A young woman in her early thirties, who had not menstruated for nearly a year, and also had severe diabetes complicated by other illnesses, began her period by the first evening of the conference. People just visiting our retreat center would immediately observe physical changes or alterations in their symptoms if they were ill. I recall one physician with severe angina walking up to me and having it stop immediately. The reverse was also true: someone with delicate respiratory function might find themselves short of breath by walking near me. In short, when consciousness is altered by a force of energy from without or from an inner opening and release, there is an immediate physical expression of this phenomenon.

But consciousness, as Jung and others have so clearly demonstrated, is not just an individual phenomenon. There is another collective level of consciousness through which all human beings (in fact, far more than human beings – all existence) are united. This collective consciousness has both a conscious and an unconscious level of expression. Through an extraordinarily rich accumulation of information in the form of dreams, legends, myths, and fairy tales, Jung demonstrated that there is a "collective unconscious," an underlying universal force, expressing itself through human experience and all human affairs. In his psychology, when an individual had found the key in their own awareness that allowed these underlying energies – he called them Archetypes – more natural expression and healing of the neurotic behavior would occur.

In my own work, I did not seek to demonstrate the existence of the collective unconscious; instead I sought to work with the energy of groups of people. In my work first with Brugh Joy, M.D., and later in my own conferences, I learned that there is an energy – a kind of group being – that can be evoked through focusing the attention of the group at a very deep level. Undoubtedly this energy is always available and is the basis of the power of mob action or, more positively, of a church con-gregation. But in my work, it is not adequate to merely identify this energy as a spiritual concept like the group soul. As a leader, I had to be able to perceive, interact with and thereby in some degree guide the unfoldment of this energy. When this occurs, a palpable field of presence (palpable to those who have been taught and thereby sensitized to its existence) develops, and I observed hundreds of instances where this energy field re-sulted in spontaneous and unexpected physical reactions. On a few occasions, the physical transformation was more than an induced menstrual cycle or new level of vitality, it was the radical and complete healing of serious illness. Whereas just being in an altered consciousness would cause some psycho-physical alteration, these radical healings were simultaneous with a fundamental transformation of the individual, similar to my own. Here, I might add that the awakening experience that I have described enabled me to explore the group energies and tremendously increased my sensitivity to this realm of sensation.

Over the years, it was the experiences of what I would like to call radical healings and transformations that became the doorway into a whole new level of inquiry and observation. First of all, I wanted to know if the circumstances of these trans - formations could be sufficiently broken down in order to perceive some continuity or pattern. Jesus had said that no man gets to the Kingdom through his own efforts and everything is possible in God. While I had no doubt that this was so, I could not deduce a formula that could be applied to produce these amazing experiences at will. Nevertheless, I felt it might be possible to perceive universal principles at work here. I hoped this might give us a greater appreciation of the wonderful, and ultimately unfathomable, mystery of Life.

Secondly, I saw another parallel between my work and Carl Jung's. Jung had realized that psychosis or neurosis was not the result of some underlying pathological or destructive force, but rather is the thwarted expression of each person's inner divinity or higher being. I too began to see that a disease such as cancer was not some horror acting upon us, which must be destroyed with surgery, radiation, chemicals and so on, but was, in reality, our own higher energetic potential expressing itself abnormally. Energy can only express itself healthfully when we have come to a profound level of balance within our individual and collective natures. We appear to be individual bodies, but this individuality is also a constant state of equilibrium between a true personal authenticity and a continuous participation with the collective energy of all humanity and all existence. To be out of balance in either the personal or collective dimensions can mean we are too large or too small for the energy moving through us. Like light shining through an irregular glass, the higher energies become terribly distorted.

It became apparent that these transformations did more than heal terrible diseases. It was as though the disease itself had been freed to a new level of expression. Said another way, it became clear to me that what we call a disease cannot be separated from the total consciousness of the individual. The healthy person isn't someone without the disease; the disease is not some abnormal addition to be eliminated. On the contrary, disease is a part of our wholeness. No matter how miserable we appear from a humanistically biased perspective, all individuals are already whole – now and always. Each of us is a complete system, and the energies of being take a particular form of expression in each of us in accordance with our own unique dynamics.

For example, a water system designed to hold one hundred pounds of pressure will inevitably leak if that pressure is greatly exceeded. To do so is a perfect expression of the wholeness of the system. On the other hand, if a one hundred pound system is exposed to five hundred pounds of pressure and does not leak or contort, or act differently in some way, this would truly be abnormal! If we want to understand the disease, we must under - stand it as part of Life itself seeking expression, through a system that is unable to contain or conduct that life except in a diseased mode. To try and label the disease as the problem misses this fundamental point.

When a person goes through a radical transformation, it is not the disease that disappears. Rather, the whole structure of his being is so totally reconfigured that the energy giving rise to the disease is freed to express in other ways. The disease simply ceases in the same way the pipes would stop leaking if we could somehow transform all of them into a material and structure designed to handle five hundred pounds of pressure.

Once I understood this and had observed a few of these major transformations (which are rare enough that it took some years before I began to see the pattern), it was not long before I realized that, far from being some dark and terrible force, diseases such as cancer are the transformational impulses seeking expression in us. This disease is not solely the result of our pollutants or our various physical, psychological or spiritual problems. Rather, it is merely an inappropriate expression of the force that seeks to right the imbalance of our times. A greater wholeness is seeking to awaken in us, greater than anything we can presently imagine or even sustain. And it is our very approach to life, as well as the profound distortions of our current individual and collective systems, which are being broken down and readied for a greater life through forces such as cancer. Cancer, heart disease and the other major illnesses of our time are not evils. If we hear their underlying message we may find them, in fact, to be God in disguise. They remind us of our capacity to express the divine impulse that is and always has been awakening in humanity.

# Maturing Into Radiant Health

## by Bill Wilkinson

In my work as a healer I know one thing: I cannot give what I do not have. What do I have, in fact? Well, forgetting whatever qualifications I may have amassed along the way (that's all lost in the past now, after all), I simply have my own experience of life in this moment. To whatever degree I am inwardly open and receptive to what is springing spontaneously forth from the current of life, I have something to offer into the healing process in myself and in another.

Life does the healing. If I myself am open to life – and that state is characterized by an easy, ongoing admission that I do *not* have all the answers stored away – then life can speak and act through me, appropriate to the needs of the moment. Healing will occur. And everyone involved in the process can enjoy the surprising way that life brings this about!

Now, in writing this chapter there is a particular challenge before me. My healing work depends entirely upon the development of an atmosphere of communion which can accommodate an intensified flow of the life current. But you and I are not in my office. I can't use my usual healing techniques. I am here writing and you are there reading. So, we'll need to improvise!

*A former director for the Canadian CABLENET system, Bill Wilkinson produced over 2,000 TV programs, several on healing, as well as hosting the TV interview series "Health Yourself" and "Options for Health." He trained in a healing process known as 'attunement,' developed over fifty years by the Society of Emissaries. Bill co-founded the Victoria Attunement Center, which serves a general clientele, as well as training doctors and allied health professionals in the essentials of learning to generate a healing atmosphere. He presently lives and practices in Aldergrove, British Columbia. Bill is the author of* Attunement with Life. *(see pg. 240)*

I will tell you a story.

Let's consider together the process of maturing into radiant health. Perhaps a unique perspective can emerge in this setting, something organic can grow in these moments, something which will encourage an increased openness towards life. Because, in the most fundamental way, that is my role as a healer. How would I describe the role? Primarily, I do two things. I help my clients remember their true identity as eternal, living beings, and I provide a charged atmosphere in which the healing partnership can develop.

In my office we often see people who have tried just about everything. They have exhausted conventional therapy. They've run the gamut of alternative and "new age" approaches. As a last resort they come to me. And what do I tell them? "Grow up!"

Now that may seem harsh. But obviously there has been a refusal to grow up in our species as a whole. And one characteristic of children is a disregard for the future. "Who cares about tomorrow, we're having too much fun right now to worry about tomorrow." So we eat what we like, we develop lifestyles of personal gratification and, like children, we release emotional torrents when we don't get what we want.

Such irresponsible behavior produces results in our bodies and our environment. These results become increasingly difficult to ignore. We'd much rather carry on playing with the steady stream of new, sophisticated toys in our global sandbox. But it seems we have a problem. The escalating chaos internally and externally is threatening our fun and games. What's to be done?

In the health field, where the disintegration becomes more personal, attention is tirelessly devoted towards finding cures. This hunt for the magic bullet is all-consuming. The latest scourge is AIDS. And of course there is a desperate hope that some "cure" for the AIDS virus can be found. This approach aims to fix up the problem without changing the cause. Childish

178

human behavior causes problems. Instead of staying childish and frantically attending to those ever-increasing problems, why not just grow up?

But, we're stubborn. Historically, we have always ignored dilemmas until the last possible moment. It is rather reminiscent of the way a child will demand to play before dinner, stretching it out to the last possible moment. I watched the movie "Star Trek IV" again recently and appreciated the wisdom in Mister Spock's observation about any race that would hunt a species (the humpback whale) to extinction. He said, "That's not logical." The reply came from someone more familiar with Twentieth Century man: "Who ever said the human race was logical?"

Obviously we haven't been. Everywhere one looks we see the results of a deliberate, willful ignoring of the warning signs. Our forests are being depleted at an alarming rate – even though we well know that we will suffocate if it goes much further. Our oceans are polluted, our air and soil are irradiated. Desert - ification intensifies...every day more species vanish forever. On it goes. And our problems increase with every new human arrival. Birth is a sweet event. But what a bitter result! As the population grows, so do the problems. And it becomes ever more evident that perhaps, from the standpoint of Mother Earth, the final solution would be the removal of the problem-causing agent: man.

Meanwhile, medical experts strive to find solutions that will ensure our survival. One might question why, considering the self-centered nature of man. What is the purpose of this human creature anyway? I recall watching television coverage of a heart transplant recipient. He was asked: "What will you do now that your life is no longer threatened?" He answered with a grateful smile, "Now I can watch football on TV again." The operation, research, etc. easily cost a million dollars. That's an expensive football game.

Is this the sole purpose for mankind: entertainment and self-satisfaction? If so, then the rest of creation must be purposeless too. Or, could it be that there *is* purpose inherent in life? It is obvious elsewhere: for instance, in the relative harmony of our solar system – the Sun doesn't strike for higher wages. But man is fundamentally out of step.

If we accept this premise, then we can see that health is inexorably tied to the fulfillment of purpose. If the human being has a purpose – which we might describe in the simplest way as the expression of life – then health would be experienced as that purpose was consistently served. Children play, and it is natural for them to be self-centered. But children are meant to grow up. Maturity comes as there is a weaning from this initial state and progressive acceptance of responsibility relative to the larger world. The responsibility is to contribute, to give.

Most have never learned to be givers. We remain childish all our lives. As physical children we demand ice cream, we want to stay up late; as adult children we want BMW's and love – even if we aren't lovable. There's a song I recall that goes: "We shouldn't have took more than we gave. Then we wouldn't be in this mess today." Perhaps that ain't good English, but it makes the point.

One might apply this perspective to the current health (disease) crisis. Traditionally we do hunt for answers outside of ourselves. But what if the solution is not a physical cure, but rather an internal change in people themselves? Is it at all plausible to suggest that what is really needed, health-wise, is more power moving through individuals? Could an increase in the power of life itself, focused with control and intelligence, meet whatever arises in the environment – our external environment or the internal one?

There are many popular stories of individuals rising to extraordinary heights to accomplish things far beyond their normal capacity. Under the pressure of a crisis circumstance they somehow access a power source and perform seeming miracles. For instance, it has been reported, in several instances, that a mother has rescued a child pinned under an automobile by lifting the vehicle with one hand and dragging the child free with the other. Here is power, much more power than generally experienced.

In my healing work I invite my clients to learn how to release this power, intelligently and under control. First of all, I receive them as inherently powerful beings. Yes, they do bring their diseases, their problems. But I am not going to heal them. They need my help in a different way, to remind them that they are personally responsible, and at least potentially capable of dealing with their own predicaments. The answer, the healing power, will spring forth from within them. I perceive each as a unique being, potentially well able to deal with the situation. They need my help, but not for healing. My assistance comes instead in the form of a reminder: "Rise up, grow up, be responsible for yourself." What I do not do is look at the diseases they bring and identify them with all that.

This approach is popular with some. Others head for the hills immediately! But I am unrelenting. My clients quickly discover that I won't let them get away with being less than what they inherently are. Originally they arrive all bound up in them - selves, oblivious to anything but their own little troubled state. I invite them to expand their vision and see with a larger perspective.

And considering our global scene together we can begin to discern some parallels. We note, for instance, that there are traditional mechanisms that maintain order in the world-at-large. Control operates through bureaucracies of one kind or another and through the threat of physical retaliation. We have governments and our countless societal "laws," our police forces, armed forces and an array of armaments – including nuclear weaponry. Also we have the legal system, another means of providing order, "fairness."

This can be seen as a macrocosm of what is present within each individual. We, too, have control systems within our bodies. For instance, we have the immune system – actually, a collaboration of many systems, providing for safety from malevolent invasions that could produce disease. This all seems normal and necessary enough. But just as we wouldn't require police forces, the legal system, etc., if people behaved themselves, our own personal state could change just as dramatically if there were correct personal function. Then all of the software and hardware could be dismantled in a moment, the very moment we begin to behave ourselves peaceably. But, as far as the world population is concerned, is that likely to happen overnight in the collective sense? It's doubtful, in fact, impossible. Change does not come that way. Change springs forth in individual experience. More specifically, change starts with the one called "me."

Now, there is some considerable encouragement to let such change come! On the global scene it is obvious that our defense systems – especially nuclear armaments – could destroy us. So we'd better learn (and quickly!) how to behave without the need for that radical deterrent. Of course the danger isn't limited to a deliberate use of nuclear weapons. There is also the possibility of "accidents." And nuclear wastes are hazardous. All this underlines the basically malevolent nature of this technology, developed originally as a means of defense, and the impossibility of keeping such powerful forces totally under control. In other words, it seems that a defensive stance can produce mechanisms potentially hazardous to the host.

Perhaps a parallel can be drawn with the human immune system. Could our own defense system represent a similar threat, on a personal level? If we are poised to fend off attack, don't we leave ourselves vulnerable to the same threats? The more powerful our "defenses" the more danger if something slips. And how easily we slip, reacting emotionally over the slightest thing. That emotion, expressed without control, affects our hormonal balance, for one thing. Now if someone in a nuclear plant or weapons facility "loses it" – either through emotional, mental or physical imbalance or through casualness or inattention – the consequences may be dire for the environment at large. One might wonder what powerful, malevolent forces are similarly released within our own bodies when we "lose it." We've all had the experience of anger, resentment....feelings that rage out of control. It never feels healthy, does it?

Our immune system develops at an early age. We have tended to see it as eternal, much in the same way that we have accepted our childish, self-centered mode as if that was all there could ever be. We say, "Forgive me, I'm only human" to explain our weaknesses. Shouldn't it be, "Forgive me, I'm still childish?" Perhaps the immune system – as a defensive mechanism – is temporary. Perhaps it is necessary to the child, as an initial assist, until the true mechanism develops in the mature adult state. In other words, the immune system would not remain forever defensive in order to do its job. It would evolve, as the rest of us does, into something else.

Comparing a baby to an adult one sees obvious, major differences. The baby can't talk, walk, create buildings or souffles. The adult can. The child's immune system functions in a certain way – we are describing it as "defensive." How would the matured immune system operate in an adult? It's anybody's guess, since so few people ever grow up and become "givers."

My own suspicion is that it would become "radiant." In other words, there would be some sort of constant outpouring of power – a steady glow – that would be sufficient to meet and deal with anything that would arise in the environment of the body.

This may be something outside the parameters of our current experience, but I believe it may be an evolutionary next step. The natural givingness of such a person, their own expression of life force, would simply extend though every level of their experience, including the ongoing internal scenario. And if the radiant power of life is powerfully present and under control throughout one's own body, what's the worry? After all, it was the power of life that created everything in the first place, even viruses. Could life be threatened by something it itself created?

Actually, "immune" means "safe." One isn't safe solely by being defensive. In fact, as long as one is defensive, one is under siege. And that is not, ultimately, a safe condition. True safety comes when one is "immune," i.e. not susceptible. One can encounter disease without becoming diseased. What then, is required in human experience to access the potential power of life, in order to develop a true security from disease? If this can be done, if in fact it is a natural part of "growing up," then one could look towards an end to fear. No more worries about "catching something."

My attunement office has provided a setting for numerous "miracles" over the years. There is nothing mysterious about it actually. One incident involved a woman with chronic neck and back pain. She had been officially classified as "handicapped" for many years. She arrived at my door and announced that surgery would be performed in two months.

I suggested we give life a chance first. She agreed. And she proceeded to let go. In the atmosphere of my office, and within the healing context we created together, she let various barriers inside herself dissolve (some related to deeply ingrained attitudes of resentment toward her husband and children). Well, some - thing happened over the next six weeks during her regular appointments. And on the day she was scheduled for surgery, she was out on the tennis court instead! No more pain. And a new set of x-rays showed that the physical problems had vanished. There was nothing left to operate on. Life had worked its magic.

I have other stories. And my colleagues have their files full. Healing occurs when certain basic requirements are met. And this has everything to do with the way the healer receives his patients, his ability to inspire them to grow up and their willingness to do it! And the first step in "doing it" is so simple: Give! That's the first simple step. Now, one might question. How? What? Well, that's revealing of the fact that one hasn't been doing it. Just give. Don't wait for a reason, a special circumstance. We all have the moment and the moment is full of our present experience. There is something to be given here and now. Simply put, we stop worrying about ourselves, we come out of ourselves into the world around us and we contribute.

This is what has been missing in the childish state. Children are self-absorbed. They see the world in terms of how it affects them. As so-called adults we have behaved the same way and we have suffered for it . The beautiful physical systems we were born with are able to sustain us in some sort of balance for just so long in an immature state. Without the radiant power of life moving through them, though, a power that should naturally increase as we increase our givingness, at some point we are left in the lurch. But it needn't happen this way. We can grow into radiance. We can give, we can let life's power express through our givingness in thought, feeling, word and action. Here is true, radiant security. And this power flowing through our expression will nourish our environment and enrich this world which is properly in our care.

185

Sometimes it is too late to help a person turn their condition around. Physical deterioration has progressed too far. They have a certain amount of time left to live and that's all there is to it. In such a case, should the healer give up? If he does, certainly the patient will. No, healing is still called for. But the goal is not to affect a cure. In these cases healing involves an orderly completion to life and a dignified death. I once attended a middle aged man who suffered from a brain tumor. He was physically unable to make it to my office. I responded to a phone call from his wife and went to their apartment. We shared a sweet, potent time. During the attunement session he experienced a temporary relief of the paralysis afflicting his left side. And his wife, who was perched on a sofa in the same room with us, felt a profound peacefulness develop within her. She had been troubled. They both had been troubled. In fact, the turmoil in their personal relationship had likely been a major contributor to the brain tumor.

He died several weeks later. But his wife called me to say that those last days had been precious. Together they had sorted through their lives and come to an experience of genuine affection for each other, something that had eluded them during their marriage. She was grateful for my one visit and thanked me for helping them appreciate the purpose of being together in those last weeks.

If it comes to this late point, that is about all we can hope to accomplish. But how about starting to let some fundamental changes come in ourselves *before* we are painted into a corner? Terminal illness can inspire deep change. But surely we can demonstrate some openness to the innate potential for personal transformation without needing a gun at our heads.

My healing work utilizes the attunement technique. And there are many types of attunement. In this setting I have used words. In my office we could use conversation, or silence with a focusing of the life current through my hands, or perhaps some music. The success of these techniques all depend upon rapport. Can we develop communion, agreement, a depth of personal connection? If so, there is the atmosphere and the opportunity for healing. It takes two, at least. Healing manifests as the life force flows through patterns of agreement between individuals. This is possible because of a connection that transcends space and time. In this space life is constantly born.

True healing occurs in this place. For instance, if you read these words and relax into the flow that created them, then you will share this healing space with me. Attunement and healing will occur.

Incidentally, all genuine healers live here. Any time you want to drop in, you are most welcome. And if you would like to stay... well, there is room for all of us here in the healing heart of life!

# The Listening Heart

## by Susanna Davis

The second floor balcony looks out over the herb garden. From there it came as a surprise one day last summer to realize that my newly designed herb garden was, in fact, in the shape of the heart! I had intended, I thought, a certain sundial effect, but somehow in the choice of plants and birdbath the aerial view was definitely heart-shaped.

My daily ritual was to stroll out to this special spot when returning home from a busy workday as a nurse-counselor-educator. I heed my sign of "No shoes beyond this point," acknowledge the guardians of the garden, three-and-a-half foot Egyptian onions, and make my way up the central path. The shape of the Evening Primroses crowding round the guardian onions, with their baby onions waving at their tops, gives the impression of a skirted medusa or gorgon to which one is obliged to speak!

Going up the pathway, the range of fragrances becomes almost overwhelming in its diversity – in turn pungent, delicate, spicy, but always haunting and delicious. By then, the sun has usually made its way behind the ancient apple tree nearby. The dappling effect created by the ripples of light dances through the various shades and shapes of foliage and flowers. Birds coast in to the birdbath for brief splashes and then sit in the apple tree

*With some twenty years experience in hospitals, public health, rehabilitation, childbirthing and teaching, Susanna Davis now practices as a community nurse. She offers holistic counseling and education in the fields of parent education and stress management. Susanna lectures widely in North America on holistic living and Therapeutic Touch. She is on the Board of Directors of the Whole Health Institute and is an active networker for the American Holistic Nurses Association. She and her two sons live with 50 other people on a rural communal farm near Toronto, Canada.*

to serenade the world. Standing in the midst of such visual and sensory beauty I am also aware of the invisible beauty – a cloud of essences like a vibrational rainbow. My breath seems to auto - matically release any accumulated tensions of my day, while a "tuning" at inarticulate levels goes on.

The outward creation of this garden followed no pre - determined idea of what the form should be. It sprang from the heart, the result of many years of conscious exploration into the inaudible and almost inarticulate realms of my Being. A creation such as this, born in an atmosphere of love and sharing with various friends, does put an articulate form on a primary internal essence. It is a living, dynamic symbol with a very radiant quality to it.

In the spiritual journey that I experience as a nurse and holistic 'artist in the healing field,' I find that I continually manifest such living symbols. They become pointers, friends with a message, that I have "heard" internally, but appreciate having objectified.

So often things that are deeply moving do not find expression in the spoken words of our day-to-day lives. Instead, this language of the heart takes form in images -- pictures, music, orperhaps just a fleeting moment in consciousness. Who has not known the thrill of new thought, a new idea seen or heard on the very edge of awareness, "Eureka!"... that moment of acknowledgment that Life has gifted us with a transcendent energy?

Many years ago, while working as a nurse in a job that involved me in people's lives as a consultant in a physical rehabilitation program, I had a major car accident. This led to a lengthy recovery, a rather humbling opportunity to be on the receiving end of a rehabilitation program, receiving treatment from various medical professionals. Somewhere in the midst of my own pain, frustration and fear of the future, I had the realization that the whole healing process somehow came down to me. "How can *I* know what to do?" was the question I asked myself with just a glimmer of confidence. That glimmer was the spark that "heard" one of Life's deep non-verbal impulses. On the basis of that impulse, I took myself away to a friend's farm and proceeded to explore "listening" to a language that was rushing out of my heart whenever I would relax and be still.

One night, soon after my arrival at this farm, there was a brilliant electrical storm blazing across the horizon outside by bedroom window. Intently, I watched the lightning shafts arcing from cloud to cloud and sky to earth. Soon, in my meditative, awe-filled state, I began to feel each crackling blast like a jolt through my own body. The awareness spread in me that *I* had moved to a new place...an unusual location in consciousness where I felt absolutely at one with the sky and earth. I was "grounding" vast energies from some invisible realm above me. I tingled with change and inner rumblings; and as the rains finally came, I found my body drenched with perspiration.

A profound sleep followed this experience, and upon wakening I knew that the healing process was well underway, controlled and directed by a source of energy beyond my mental understanding. The fuzziness and fear had disappeared and – miraculously to me at the time – in their place was a calm assurance that everything was just fine! Day by day a course of action unfolded in my receptive awareness. It required that I take certain steps, many in direct contradiction to the medical models in which I had been trained.

Part of the recovery process was time spent in my friend's garden. I poured my enthusiasm and thankfulness for being alive and on the move into the care of vegetable and herbal plants, which provided a substantial part of my daily diet. One day I came across a slug and garden snail "village" living under some rotting rhubarb leaves. Picking up a discarded snail shell reminded me of my former seashell collections, and the vision of one large shell, in particular. The image of this shell floated to the surface of my consciousness during meditative times. I took the little snail shell as a pocket talisman and let myself explore its message. It was an outer symbol of something my heart yearned to say. It seemed to speak of my new-found confidence, that my direction had a spiraling movement to it, that cycles would come around again, and that *my journey was the important thing,* not some supposed destination.

This had proven to be the basis of my nursing practice. I "listen" with others to what the heart would say in its longing to open more fully to Life. At any given crisis point in living, whether it is an acute or debilitating illness, or mental or emotional disturbances, each person has the key to his or her own starting point in the healing process. For one elderly man, whose lungs and heart were diseased, the key was a passion for animals and birds. He kept a poster of a kitten hanging on a bar with the caption: "Hang in there" on his wall. For several weeks he struggled with a message he felt coming to him through the poster until one day he said, "I need to let the kitten fall. I don't have to 'hang in there' anymore!" At that point we began to seriously plan for his death. He was ready to make that step and do it fearlessly and joyfully.

Another man with a recurrent brain tumor decided he needed a totally new approach to his health/disease. He was a left-brain centered, logical man, a banker. We contracted to do some visualization work, which eventually put him in touch with his inner "messengers." He took up drawing and collage-making, which began to reveal symbols of his past, present and future. In the process he discovered a sense of wholeness and beauty that was completely new in his experience.

In another instance, I was doing palliative care therapeutic touch with a 12-year old girl dying of cancer. Her family was reluctant to discuss any of the deeper aspects of the dying process. However, one day the younger sister drew a beautiful rainbow heart and rainbow butterfly to show me how she and her sister felt. In her symbolism, her dying sister was the butterfly and she herself was the heart. It was a privilege to acknowledge her deep "knowing"; this young 9-year-old provided a very stable spiritual presence for her family through her sister's subsequent death and funeral.

In my work I frequently use Therapeutic Touch: the laying on of hands experience of balancing and attuning the body's energy field. I have found that many children call it the "rainbow massage." Such symbols have a vast meaning for us as human beings. The human heart that has been constricted and hurting from some past experience does not always release its tensions easily. I have found, however, that this same heart will melt, release and open anew if engaged in a ceremony using meaningful symbols appropriate to the individual.

A mother, whose baby had died, wanted to create a "leave-taking ceremony" after we had had several bereavement coun - seling sessions. She chose several symbols for the constricted heart; for example, a copy of the family tree, symbolizing her guilt at not producing an heir, a letter, and a bill of money. This and other symbols she burned. The ashes she put in a hole that she and the father had dug, and there she planted a flowering shrub. After this simple ceremony she looked like a new woman, with a new sense of place and celebration. The many physical symptoms she had had: recurrent headaches, chest pains and aching arms, disappeared completely.

The heart does speak most eloquently if we listen with our inner ear. For me, it is in these realms that nursing service primarily lies. Nursing reaches out to the hearts of others to assist as midwives in the birthing of new consciousness. Nurses have frequent opportunities to facilitate the transformation of the experience of discomfort and disease into one of growth, renewal and opportunity. Let the heart speak clearly, and it will touch the world around!

# Doctors, Patients & Inner Wellness

## by Bernard S. Siegel, M.D.
## with
## Barbara H. Siegel, B.S.

In an intuitive way, I believe from the time life begins one is aware of the heart of healing, of the fact that it is not mechanical or remedy-oriented. A mother's touch, a kiss, or a doctor's phone call suddenly bring relief. We begin to become aware of the interplay of psyche and soma.

From the outset one must understand that all healing is scientific. The problem is science's inability to measure or document what occurs. A typical example is the so-called spontaneous remission of an incurable cancer. I would rather have this spontaneous event retitled creative or self-induced healing, or a hard work miracle. The former title turns aside the health practitioner's curiosity since it doesn't fit his scientific knowledge or his belief system. Solzhenitsyn wrote of self-induced healing in *Cancer Ward* (Farrar, Straus, Giroux, 1969):

> Kostoglotov...[said]..."we shouldn't behave like rabbits and put our complete trust in doctors. For instance, I'm reading this book." He picked up a large, open book

*Bernard S. Siegel, M.D., F.A.C.S. is a graduate of Cornell Univ. (M.D. 1957). He has had a private practice in general and pediatric surgery since 1962 in New Haven, Connecticut. He resides nearby with his wife, Barbara Siegel, B.S., who is editor and co-author of their articles and five children. He is founder of a therapy program called Exceptional Cancer Patients. He has numerous affiliations with medical and psychological associations, and is well known as a speaker at workshops and presentations nationwide. He is the author of the bestselling book* Love, Medicine & Miracles. *(see page 240)*

This chapter is taken from an article appearing in *The American Theosophist* entitled "The Spiritual Aspects of the Healing Arts" and is reprinted by permission of the author and the publisher, The Theosophical Society of America.

from the window sill. "Abrikosov and Stryukov, *Pathological Anatomy,* medical school textbook. It says here that the link between the development of tumors and the central nervous system has so far been very little studied. And this link is an amazing thing! It's written here in so many words." He found the place. "'It happens rarely, but there are cases of self-induced healing.' You see how it's worded? Not recovery through treatment, but actual healing. See?"

There was a stir throughout the ward. It was as though "self-induced healing" had fluttered out of the great open book like a rainbow-colored butterfly for everyone to see, and they all held up their foreheads and cheeks for its healing touch as it flew past.

"Self-induced." said Kostoglotov, laying aside his book. He waved his hands, fingers splayed..."That means that suddenly for some unexplained reason the tumor starts off on the opposite direction! It gets smaller, resolves and finally disappears! See?"

They were all silent, gaping at the fairy tale. That a tumor, one's own tumor , the destructive tumor which had mangled one's whole life, should suddenly drain away, dry up and die by itself?

They were all silent, still holding their faces up to the butterfly. It was only the gloomy Podduyev who made his bed creak and, with a hopeless and obstinate expression on his face, croaked out, "I suppose for that you need to have...a clear conscience."

To understand how to fit spirituality into the healing process or to recognize its place, let me take a step back and describe present medical training.

Young men and women are accepted into medical school based upon their ability to take tests and accumulate knowledge. (Hopefully they also have an interest in people.) They are then taught about disease and its treatment. Little if any time is given to the study of their feelings and how to deal with people.

They are oriented into a failure system, meaning, we fill our time, offices, and hospitals with people who don't do well, and we do more to them if their first treatment fails. We fight disease with the poor patient as the battleground. If a patient does well, we do not see him again, and if he gets well when he is not supposed to, we tell him it isn't necessary for him to return, or ignore his recovery as being mystical. Any good business would study success, but medicine ignores it. We should be knocking on survivors' doors saying "Why didn't you die when you were supposed to?" We should be teaching the messages all survivors know. By survivors, I mean survivors of disease, concentration camps, tragic life events, or other disasters.

The students become more mechanics than healers. They are taught what to do to people who are sick and little about why people get sick. They are, therefore, given the unspoken role of lifesavers. Again, this sets them up for failure, since everyone ultimately dies. The healthcare provider, therefore, withdraws from the patient so the eventual failures will be less painful. He, therefore, does not become aware of what truly occurs when one lives with disease. He has little contact with the healing process or its absence. In this setting the idea that the disease can become a motivator for change is overlooked.

After going through the whole medical education process and starting my own practice, I found myself feeling very unhappy as a mechanic-lifesaver. I knew from my childhood that there was more to the healing process. I knew doctors were not always right in sentencing people to death. My mother was told not to become pregnant or she would die. A case of hyperthyroidism had her weighing ninety pounds and an obstetrician thought a pregnancy would be life threatening.

To make a long story short, she found another obstetrician who agreed to work with her if she gained weight. After she gained thirty pounds she conceived. I was born and the hyper - thyroidism disappeared. It was hard for me not to be accepted and loved by my parents after a beginning like that. In any event, this love was a handicap for a doctor, as it didn't fit into the medical model to which I was exposed. Nowhere in medical school was any time spent discussing why one becomes a doctor. I practiced medicine for a decade with a heavy heart trying to fit love and spirituality into my practice. I inquired into other professions for a possible career change until a cancer pa - tient made me aware of the people I was caring for. As strange as this may sound I saw diseases in the waiting room, not people. Once I began to orient my practice to people, my life and my practice changed. Patients came in and said, "Now I can talk to you." When my belief system changed it was safe for them to talk about the spiritual and mystical events related to their illnesses.

Initially, I sent letters to one hundred patients inviting them to begin meeting in groups to deal with their lives with an holistic approach. I expected hundreds of responses and had only twelve. I realized that of the people I saw and see with chronic or catastrophic illness, about twenty percent are the truly exceptional patients or survivors. This may vary in different living areas depending on how independent and how used to participating in their own lives they are. The exceptional patient or survivor is willing to take responsibility for his problem.

To learn the kind of person I was dealing with I began to ask four simple questions. 1) Do you want to live to be 100? (A simple question about feeling in control and looking forward to life.) 2)What does your disease mean to you?(Is it a challenge or a death sentence?) 3)Why did you need the illness? (What is it providing you with? — nurturing and love, as do our sick days at work?) 4) What happened in the year or two before you became sick? (This lets the patients know how they participate in an illness by not meeting their needs. It makes them responsible for change if they wish to accept the responsibility.)

The mechanic would treat the illness and not look at who was sick. The healer/teacher says: "who are you? Who were you? And what brings you to this point?" We have the opportunity to lead people on new pathways to help them with their rebirth.

Illness or pain is a message to change. In an all inclusive way I used the phrase, "Everyone has his cancer, either emotional or physical." From this ground we have the option to either promote change and healing, or see it as a catastrophe or death sentence. I choose the former, and I offer it to my patients.

Since the medical profession is failure-oriented, it tends to say to people,"don't ask why you became ill"; it will make you feel that it is your fault, that you are a failure. I say the illness must be seen as a message to redirect your life, and, within this transformation, healing occurs.

I know the power of this transformation and the knowledge our inner voices, intuition, or unconscious minds can provide. For years I ignored it but kept getting a powerful personal message to uncover something. As a mechanic, therefore, I went to the barber and had my head shaved. Of course, having a bare head didn't solve the problem.

One teacher who helped me was Elizabeth Kubler-Ross. At a workshop, she interpreted a spontaneous drawing of mine. It shows a fish out of water (a spiritual symbol) and a mountain covered with snow. (A white crayon utilized to portray snow on an already white piece of paper represents a symbolic coverup.) What this drawing did was to show me what needed to be un -

covered was not my head but my love and spirituality, and then I would no longer feel like a fish out of water. A new world opened up where a mechanic could exist no longer with his old belief system. By bringing this new belief system into my practice, my world and the world of my patients changed. I realized that mind and body communicate by a symbolic language and consequently I now utilize dreams and drawings as a regular part of my therapeutic and diagnostic approach. Mind, body, and spirit are considered as one unit. Being a highly skilled mechanic is important but true healing occurs only when psyche, soma, and spirit are integrated.

When you use this new approach patients begin to share with you the life events prior to their becoming ill. They realize the illness allows them to say "no" to demands they would have felt obligated to fulfill. However, when I offer people options for getting well most prefer the mechanical, "Cut it out; I can get a babysitter" approach instead of one of changing their lifestyle. They say exercise and meditation may change family routine and the spouse will be angry.

We would rather be ruined than changed.
We would rather die in our dread
than climb the cross of the moment and
let our illusions die.
        W.H. Auden

The illness gives me a chance to teach people about unconditional love: giving with no expectations because one chooses to give. Discipline and saying no are permitted between two people sharing this love. It is the conditional love upon which most of us are brought up, that leads to illness. We never get all the thanks and praise we would like. When we are giving unconditional love, it restores us and provides us with a reason for living. Physical handicap or illness does not interfere with the ability to give love. Invariably the love is returned to us without our asking because people see the change and want to be closer to this newfound peace.

Many of my patients who are physically quite ill, some near death, wonder why they still have so many visitors. I explain to them that their spirit is very much alive and that 'terminal' is a state of mind. Their spirit and love attract others because the others see life, not death, and therefore are comfortable in their presence.

In 1926 Elida Evans in her book entitled *A Psychological Study of Cancer* said, "Cancer is a symbol, as most illness is, of something going wrong in the patient's life, a warning to him to take another road." Those who take this new road find a new life, exceed expectations and sometimes are cured of incurable illness. The new lifestyle is the goal, not physical well-being. The latter is the traditional medical approach.

The physician can be a spiritual leader and help people be reborn. These same patients are not upset with you for not healing them physically, but they actually thank you for the new life and ability to love. They feel this way because you indeed have made them eternal in the only way possible.

The secret to being eternal is love. Thornton Wilder said,"and we ourselves shall be loved for a while and then forgotten but the love will have been enough, even memory is not necessary for love, there is a land of the living and a land of the dead and the bridge is love." It can be said in another way: to die but not to perish, that is eternity. Love teaches us how not to perish.

There is eternal life through love, yet part of the reason physicians have no need to deal with this problem is that, unconsciously, they believe doctors don't get sick or die. (This is an unconscious reason for many to become doctors, but it is never addressed during medical training.)

There is a massive denial which keeps doctors from feeling what their patients feel and, therefore, from needing to face illness and death. For those who are up against these problems the physician has little advice. When I asked God what to do when confronted with a patient with a serious illness who I could help or God could heal, He said, "Render unto the doctor what is the doctor's and unto God what is God's."

One patient, when confronted with a dismal future leading to the grave, asked her doctor (who made the prognosis), "But what can I do?" He replied, "You only have a hope and prayer." She asked, "How do I hope and pray?" And he said "I don't know, that's not my line." With my help she has learned to hope and pray. She has transcended her physical illness and her fears and now goes to her doctor to bring him life and love. He, in - cidentally, has become very busy making notes about her exceptional course.

Doctors' invulnerability is one aspect of the problem, and another is what I have labeled the "war and peace" aspect of medicine. The doctor sees God as coming in only when he feels helpless or hopeless, an unfortunate loss of the spiritual component of healing. Spirituality should not be relegated to "helpless" cases because it provides exceptional results and has cured the medically incurable.

Where can spirituality fit into a war on disease? How does the greatest healing power in the universe adjust to killing? Can healing occur in this environment? Listen to the language of medicine's war on illness: we kill, insult, assault, blast, and poison you and your body. All these are words with which doctors are comfortable. Tests have shown that eighty percent of all people are not comfortable killing, unless they have to kill to save the lives of loved ones. Neither are we comfortable in killing disease, since it is a part of us. There is only a small percentage of patients who are comfortable being aggressive towards something residing within.

The disease should be seen as a part of a personal growth process. We can use our white blood cells to consume the disease (nourish themselves on the disease) and we can grow psychologically because of the disease. This process then creates immune system changes which can lead us to healing and new life.

I believe diseases are a response to loss and have often thought of the comparison to a salamander. Salamanders, incidentally, have very few cancers but do have the ability to regenerate and we have the opposite potential.

If a salamander has a loss it grows a new part. If we have a loss we grow a cancer or generate a disease. As one of my pa - tients said; "I grew it to fill the emptiness inside of me."

If a salamander has an extensive cancer and its tail is cut off a new tail grows and the cancer returns to normal cells. By instructing my patients to grow I hope to stop the growth within them, restore them to normal and open a pathway to physical, mental, and spiritual health.

My therapeutic goal has more to do with peace of mind than physical healing. Why? Because that is the stuff of which miracles are made. W.C. Ellerbroek, former surgeon and now psychiatrist, feels that cancer miracles occur only when people are moribund or practically so. That is when they give up the despair and the healing process begins. (He has over five dozen well documented cases at last communication.) How sad to wait until one is almost dead to resolve conflict.

I try to teach this message to my patients. Live with a sense of time limitation. Decide things based upon the value of your time. Say what needs to be said, resolve conflicts and share openly the love you feel. What happens then?

One of my hospitalized patients told me she felt like dying. I said, "That's all right but please share this feeling with your children and your parents. They don't know how badly you feel." I came back after the weekend to see her and she looked wonderful. She had on make-up, a suit and her wig. I said, "What happened?" She answered, "I told my children how I felt. I told my parents how I felt and then I felt so good I didn't want to die." She was discharged from the hospital. I have seen other patients who were expected to die resolve their conflicts and be discharged with, as one patient said, "incredible energy." That is the power of love which resides in each of us. I have watched those who have learned to live leave their bodies. It is a peaceful, pain-free process in which no time is really spent dying. It is a letting go. For this to occur two basic conditions must be met: The lifesaver/doctor must be instructed when to stop and loved ones must give permission to the individual with the illness to fight or not. Finally, those with the illness are given permission to die when they no longer feel they are "living." Their survivors share their love and grief and the knowledge that they will be able to go on because of the shared love. This allows the life and death decision to be made by the individual free from the "don't die" messages we often give each other. If we give "don't die" messages death becomes a failure, something that must occur in secret when the loved ones and lifesavers are not present.

This then allows the individual the choice of a time to die and people with whom the event is shared. It allows family members to say, "It's all right to go." It allows them to see their loved one take one breath and die.

Being present at such a death makes one aware that it is a transition. The spirit leaves the body, the cocoon, and moves on. Scientists will describe this as the parasympathetic nervous system slowing and stopping bodily functions, but it doesn't look scientific, it looks spiritual when you are there.

> We shall not cease from exploration and
> the end of all our exploring will be to arrive where
> we started from and know that place for the first time.

> T.S. Eliot

Just as Solzhenitsyn in his book *Cancer Ward* sees spontaneous healing as a rainbow colored butterfly, so his unconscious knows that to heal one must deal with one's life spectrum (the rainbow) and shed the cocoon and become a new person (a butterfly) with a "clear conscience" as Podduyef says in the book.

This spontaneous change can more easily occur when we open to God's healing energy. Once a patient of mine returned to the office free of an incurable cancer and said,"I left my troubles to God." I now had a therapy to share with others.

However, if God said to you, "Be happy!" what would most of us do? We would ask for an exception in our case. Why? Because if God only knew our life and troubles He wouldn't ask us to be happy; He would allow us to be victims and an exception to His rule of happiness. If one conceives of God as an intelligent, loving light, and if one opens to this light, true healing of mind, body and spirit can occur.

I have long felt the absence of God from our hospitals. Notice the absence of signs of spirituality in a hospital not run by a religious order. One of my associates, Richard Selzer, a surgeon and writer, shares my feeling eloquently in his short story "Absence of Windows." He states, "I very much fear that, having bricked up our windows, we have lost more than the breeze; we have severed a celestial connection." In this article he was discussing the removal of the windows from the operating room.

How do we reestablish this connection? Obviously not by bringing windows back but by creating a healing, spiritual environment. I personally use music as a way of reestablishing this connection. Since biblical times this quality of music has been known. It creates a mental state conducive to healing, as well as a greater awareness of the true nature of healing and our common source.

It is my belief that music creates a healing rhythm within the body, a harmony of all parts. I believe dreams and drawings reveal the symbolism of this rhythm. Healthy organs have their natural vibration based upon their molecular structure.

Disease changes this rhythm; disharmony occurs and it registers in the mind. To convert this to mental awareness symbols are used. If we pay attention to these symbolic messages we can diagnose disease at an earlier stage and, hopefully, learn to send healing messages or symbols back to the body. Historically, Carl Jung diagnosed physical illness based upon patients' dreams. And I have been able to do so with dreams or drawings. Frequently the patients are already aware of the dream contents' meaning and are simply sharing it with me. My patients' dreams and drawings reveal our common or collective unconscious, our common origin, our shared beginning with all men, and so the source of healing is of the same origin for us all.

What are the changes which create a healing environment? They start with the introduction of laughter, music, love, forgiveness and acceptance, all coming after a release of resentment, conflict and despair. Every cell in the body is then involved in the healing process. When we laugh every cell laughs. When we love our immune system feels the most vibrant life-message it can receive and fights for our life. I say choose this course not in an attempt to try to live forever, but rather because of the beauty it brings to your life. It is God's work. If you choose to love you are a success. You will have days when you will disappoint yourself for not loving enough, but forgive and go on. It is the pilgrimage which is important, and what we encounter along the way; not the necessity of reaching "sainthood" but striving towards it.

Emmett Fox has said:

"There is no difficulty that enough love will not conquer; no disease that enough love will not heal; no door that enough love will not open; no gulf that enough love will not bridge; no wall that enough love will not throw down; no sin that enough love will not redeem... It makes no difference how deeply seated may be the trouble; how hopeless the outlook; how muddled the tangle; how great the mistake. A sufficient realization of love will dissolve it all. If only you could love enough you would be the happiest and most powerful being in the world."

To me the last sentence is the key. Some of us may feel like failures if we don't accomplish everything he suggests, but it is the exceptional person who chooses to attempt it and knows how hard it is. Yet it is this difficulty that allows us through shared pain to help each other. The person who chooses to be the family failure or life's victim is no help to others. He is always dying. Lovers are always living and feeling. Rilke has said, "Do not believe that he who seeks to comfort you lives untroubled among the simple and quiet words that sometimes do you good. His life has much difficulty and sadness and remains far behind yours. Were it otherwise he would never have been able to find those words."

To choose love is to bring into effect the spiritual healing force and source of life. I choose to live by Teilhard de Chardin's words: "Someday, after we have mastered the winds, the waves, the tides, and gravity, we shall harness for God the energies of love. Then, for the second time in the history of the world man will have discovered fire."

One could go on quoting the great men of history referring to the power of love and not convince anyone. Let us rather believe and act upon it, and see the change that then occurs in our lives. Science teaches us to see in order to believe. Spirit says believe and you will see. I know the latter to be true.

In my early years of practice, patients did not share with me their healing or out-of-body or life-after-life experiences and I wondered if any of this was true. When I changed, my patients changed. Of course it was my change. Now they were free to share with a believer: a blind patient seeing as he watched his own resuscitation -- an amputee being whole again and describing the beauty of where we are all going. Many of my patients have shared these incredibly moving and beautiful experiences that remove fear and fill their lives with love; their bodies being God's gifts they use them to the fullest before choosing to move on.

One stops judging what I call "spiritual flat tires," which are those events that delay you in order for you to meet someone you wouldn't have met if you hadn't had the "flat tire" event. I ask you to believe and see what occurs in your life. Live with a sense of time limitation and, because of it, feel comfortable to say 'no' without guilt. Love, be selfless, childlike, and see the love returned.

I can testify that my attempt to help twelve of my patients in our first "exceptional cancer patient" group has led me to receive love from several continents. I subsequently have had the opportunity to love and heal so many more, including medical students and physicians, who are opening to this new light all because I wanted to give something to the world.

I consider Carl Jung's work one of my greatest resources. He said: "Your picture of God or your idea of immortality is atrophied, consequently your psychic metabolism is out of gear." "Every problem, therefore brings the possibility of a widening of consciousness, but also the necessity of saying goodbye to childlike unconsciousness and trust in nature."

It is time for medicine to get its psychic metabolism in gear and cast aside the guilt caused by leaving the Garden of Eden (trust in nature). We must become a success-oriented healing discipline using the patient's illness as the "ticket of admission." Then, not mechanics but healers and teachers will redirect their lives on a healing pathway. You might ask me why I am still a surgeon. I still see my mechanical skills as a way of buying time for the healing process to happen. I know I can operate on patients and see them have less pain and fewer complications when we are a healing team, utilizing faith in ourselves, our treatment and our spiritual faith. Despite all that has been said up to this point, as a surgeon my feet remain on the ground. Patients do have complications, and some die but in the process I still have something to offer them. The mechanic would be at a loss and, unable to handle the situation, might desert them.

A traditional Indian saying that sums up my sentiments: "When you were born, you cried and the whole world rejoiced. Live such a life, that when you die the whole world cries and you rejoice." To accomplish this requires only a short time. As long as one is alive it can be accomplished, change can occur. Richard Bach, the author of *Jonathan Livingston Seagull*, has said, "Here is a test to find if your mission on earth is finished: If you're alive it isn't." Many children who die give the gift of love to their parents and it lasts them a lifetime. Others choose a lifetime of hate because of a similar loss. I can only ask you to choose life.

# Seven Steps to Healing Power

## by Joseph Sweere

"To some has been given the gift of healing,"according to the scriptures. (I Corinthians 12:9) Just what is this "gift"? What is this unique power? To whom is it given and under what circumstances?

All healing stems from a single source: love. Wellness is a manifestation of that source, and healers are purveyors of love.

One of the primary causes of disease is stress. Stress is the result of conflict. Conflict is the result of fear. Only the mind can create fear. Both health and disease came from thought and both are the result of free will. Choosing one will abolish the other. By choosing fear, humans reject the miracle of health; by choosing health, disease is overcome.

There are many elements which constitute a measure of our power to heal. I have chosen these seven which I believe are particularly important.

## Communication

In simple terms the word "communication" can he defined as "to understand and be understood." To understand – to fully understand – therefore implies that you have knowledge, aware -

Joseph J. Sweere, D.C., is a 1961 graduate of Northwestern College of Chiropractic. He is the director and coordinator of postgraduate training in chiropractic industrial consulting for Northwestern College of Chiropractic and has written and lectured nationally and internationally on this subject. He is the founder of the International Academy of Chiropractic Industrial Consultants. He practiced chiropractic in Owatonna, Minnesota for twenty-five years and is currently director of the Department of Occupational and Community Health at Northwestern College of Chiropractic in Bloomington.

ness and wisdom, with a total appreciation of your patient and his or her difficulties.

To fully understand implies that you are a master diag - nostician, which converts to accurate decisions regarding the ap - propriate treatment plan. Assuming the balance of the definition has been accomplished, "to be understood" implies that your patient has conveyed his or her understanding and willingness to participate in the treatment plan. From this, you can see that the doctor who is the best communicator will also become the best healer.

Communication is essentially the result of three levels of stimulation: audible, visual and tactile. The doctor who uses the right words at the right time, who truly listens, and who uses his sense of touch in a truly healing manner, will be a genuine blessing to his or her patient.

You are aware that the word "doctor," in addition to meaning "learned person," also means "teacher." Of necessity therefore, one must become an "educator" of health to become a true doctor.

Obviously, all education is founded upon the premise of communication. Within the substance of communication, there - fore, resides the foundation of healing. It is a first step, without which the second step cannot be taken.

## Constructive Imagery

As we now understand, humans think largely in pictures. Thoughts and ideas are like mental images. The skillful phys - ician, therefore, has the ability to construct mental pictures or images of healing in the belief system of the patient. This phen - omenon is known a "visualization" or "constructive imagery" and represents a powerful tool in the process of healing.

In the scriptures, Matthew quoted the master healer, Jesus, who made the profound statement, "As a man thinketh and believeth in his heart, so it shall be." (Matt. 9:29) Note that he did not say, "so it *might* be"...nor "so it shall *sometimes* be." He said, "so it shall be." This suggests there are no exceptions. In other words, whatever we *think about and believe* becomes a reality in our lives.

What the patient thinks about and believes is critically impor - tant. The clinician has a significant effect on the patient's belief system, which, in many instances, can make the difference between the persistence of illness and the attainment of health.

Healing is not magic. It is the result of predictable laws of cause and effect. Health is the result of positive influences and sickness the result of negative influences. Healing cannot take place in a negative environment. It is imperative, therefore, that health professionals create a positive healing environment for their patients. This is done primarily through the thoughts and attitudes that are held by the individuals who occupy the space where the healing is to take place. Without being consciously aware of it, the patient is able to 'feel' the vibrations of the energy field that is created by our thoughts and feelings. We therefore have the opportunity to start the 'healing process simply by holding the appropriate thoughts and mental pictures in our minds. Do not discount the value of this counsel. This step is so simple, that many of us might be tempted to ignore it.

We should never even attempt to heal when our attitude is negative. We cannot give what we do not have. Trying to do so results in frustration for the healer as well as for the patient. Our first task is to radiate the energies of enthusiasm, optimism, hope and joy. These are truly healing vibrations and are our greatest allies in developing the 'power to heal.'

# Caring

The next element in unlocking our power to heal is our ability to genuinely care about our patients. It is obviously important to care for your patient. All doctors do that. The wise doctor, the one who understands something about healing, knows that it is likewise critically important to care *about* them.

In other terms, this means that the most effective doctor is the one who cares the most and is able to truly love his or her patients. Usually, loving your patients is a natural process and relatively easy to do, however we find that there are patients who are not particularly lovable. There are those who are disagreeable, those who are demanding, those who have B.O., those that are 100 pounds overweight, and those who smoke four packs of cigarettes and drink 25 cups of coffee every day. There are those who are ungrateful and those who skip their appointments. There are those who forget to pay their fees and those who will take you and your services for granted. So, loving our patients is not always easy!

When we find it difficult to love, however, it is important to remember that we can only begin to love when we begin to *tolerate.* Tolerance brings forgiveness, understanding and pa - tience. While difficult to believe, the lowly emotion of tolerance is the first stage of loving. The true measure of tolerance and the first step in the process of learning to love is learning to be non-judgmental.

"Love" is another definition of "healing." Sages throughout history have assured us that it is the most powerful force in the universe.

When we express love it is very, very powerful, and by some great miracle, invariably results in healing for the doctor as well as for the patient!

## Consistency

Consistency represents an important element of our power to heal. Healing is not a 'nine-to-five' occupation. Patients do not become ill or injured at our convenience. Our happiness as a healer and clinician will be that of service to our fellow humans. Success is spelled 's-e-r-v-i-c-e.' Our ability must be balanced by our availability.

There is a saying that goes like this: "Do what you *ought* to do, not what you want to do, and after you have done what you ought to do for long enough, you will find that what you ought to do, is also what you want to do."

## Confidence

Confidence is simply a matter of deciding to live your *faith,* rather than living your *fear*. We owe it to ourselves and to our patients to develop total professional competence and confidence so that our faith is manifest and easily demonstrated in all that we say and do. Worry, fear, anxiety and negative thinking are as one. Root them out of your life. They are the basis for most of the illness and misery in the world.

It has been said that worrying is a sin! It is a grave insult to God; it is like slapping Him in the face and saying: "I don't trust you."

## Character

The sixth element of healing power is character. This simply means *integrity*. By living the integrity we *earn* the love and respect of our patients and our peers, but most importantly, we

217

earn the love and respect of the most important person in our life: that person in the mirror!

In every branch of the healing arts the need is for pro - fessionals who live and practice with integrity, moral conduct and ethical professional deportment. Our individual and collec - tive future rest upon this single premise. Reflecting upon this, it is my conviction that eventually, individuals, as well as insti - tutions, get exactly what they deserve – no more and no less.

That which is in the patient's best interests is also in the doctor's best interests. Likewise, that which is in the best inter - ests of the public health is in the best interests of chiropractic. I believe that when chiropractors universally recognize this simple truth and genuinely put it into practice, the great majority of our problems as a profession will disappear.

## Collected Wisdom

In the works of writers like Emmet Fox, Eric Berne, Kahlil Gibran, Norman Vincent Peale, Dale Carnegie, Og Mandino, Napoleon Hill, and Robert Schuller we find a collection of instruction and inspiration which may remind us of our goals and keep our eyes focused on the great principles of living and healing. The writers and philosophers can help us remember and understand some of the following principles, which have been so powerful in my life and in the lives of millions:

Retain a sense of wonder, of awe. Remain curious. Keep im - proving. Take chances for good. The greater the risk, the greater the reward. Nothing worthwhile is ever conflict free. Keep trying. People do not fail, they just stop trying.

If you are going to do it at all, do it with gusto. Do it with enthusiasm. Dare to live passionately!

Realize that the secret of success is helping others to succeed. Success in cards, as in life, comes not from holding good cards, but from playing your cards well.

When times are tough, remember what Robert Schuller taught us: "Tough times never last, but tough people do!"

Develop a keen sense of humor. Laugh and produce laughter. It is good for you. Don't take yourself, nor life, too seriously. The soul seeks release from the relentless and deafening demands of the ego.

Keep learning. "If you think education is expensive, consider the price of ignorance!"

Beware of 'panaceas.' Avoid being gullible in matters of heal - ing. Healers are scientists with social responsibilities.

Pay attention. Albert Einstein said, "The difference between mediocrity and genius is the ability to focus one's attention."

Be grateful. Schopenhauer said: "We seldom think of what we have, but always what we lack. This tendency is the greatest tragedy on earth – it has caused more misery than all the wars and diseases in the history of man!"

In final summary, remember that Jesus said: "Love God, love your neighbor and love yourself"..."this then, is the essence of the law..." (Matt. 22:37-40)

The practice of healing should never be called "work." Remember the inspirational words of the renowned Canadian physiologist, Hans Selye, who stated that, in order to avoid stress in our lives, we ought to find a work which is so satisfying, so enjoyable and enriching to our daily experience that we would not want to call it "work."

If we desire to heal the sick, we must become well in body, mind and spirit, doing whatever we must do to become healthy. Physicians of every discipline who are healthy are optimally effective. They have overcome fear in their lives. Having done so, they are of assistance in removing fear in the lives of their patients. When healers are afraid, they are deceived and their minds cannot serve the good which resides within their heart. The heart of an individual healer determines his or her personal health as well as the health of his or her patient. The feelings which reside within the hearts of all healers, in large measure, will determine the health of the world.

# From Outer Disease to Inner Perfection

## by Dr. Alan Sherr

Mary came into the office about three months ago, over-weight, pale and fearful. She was referred to me by a good friend, a psychologist, who was counseling her. For about two years she had been experiencing neck pain and radiating dis-comfort into her left arm and back. Over the years she had visited many doctors, including chiropractors, finding only tem-porary relief. On our first visit I was struck by her fear and a tone which could be described as one of resignation. It seemed as though she didn't care whether or not she felt better. To start with, I asked her why she had come. If I was correct in my first impression, it wouldn't make sense for her to see me, since she didn't appear to want to get well anyway.

It's funny that people go to doctors to get well, yet they think it's normal to be sick. If it's normal to be sick, why go to a doctor in the first place?!

"Mary, if you don't want to get well, going to the doctor sure doesn't make sense," I said. She indicated in a lethargic tone and with a fleeting gaze (unable to make eye contact) that she came because of a recommendation; my friend thought I could help her: "He told me that you were different than the other doctors I have gone to."

I asked her many questions and discovered that she had been

Alan Paul Sherr, D.C. is a graduate of New York Chiropractic College (1980). He is a full-time practicing chiropractor and co-founder of the Huntington Chiropractic and Wellness Center in Huntington, New York. Dr. Sherr has been a member of the Whole Health Institute since its inception and is now a member of its International Board as Northeast Regional Director. He lectures on a wide variety of topics relating to health care and its implications. He lives with his wife and two children in Northport, New York..

overweight most of her life; she had been a school teacher for 20 years; she had been diagnosed as having diabetes, and at the present time she and her husband were not getting along. She had been in therapy for a number of years, both with a psych - iatrist, and now with a psychologist. She had tried all sorts of remedies and approaches, including dietary changes, exercise and attitude alterations. But all these produced only temporary relief. After a period of treatment, all of her old habits and symp - toms would reappear.

I have had numerous experiences with cases just like this over the years – a person comes into the office with a physical (structural) and/or organic problem after trying medical doctors, drugs and surgery, chiropractors and adjustments, exercise, nu - trition and supplements, and attitudinal therapy. Their problems would be temporarily reduced for short periods of time. It seemed as though the therapies were useful, but, in and of them - selves, they weren't the answer. Both conventional treatments and alternative, holistic approaches worked, but only temporar - ily.

So, here was Mary, reliving the scenario that I had come across over and over again. It was quite apparent that the same approach would not work. What could I offer her that could assist her in making a permanent change?

Mary's case reminded me of a story I heard a few years ago. A woman came to visit her chiropractor. She looked old and haggard, and was grossly arthritic and deformed. She was in constant pain and had exhausted all conventional means of treatment. The doctor discovered that she hated her husband and that her life was generally miserable. He indicated that he would attempt to help her, and proceeded to give her adjustments, always indicating to her that she had the power to heal herself and that he would attempt to assist her in discovering this. One day, after a few months had passed, the woman came in without pain! She had a joyous glow in her eyes and the arthritic crippling appeared greatly reduced. He asked her what had happened and she told the doctor that she had started having an 'affair.' It was apparent that the woman saw her lover as the one who helped her get better. Though she had never appeared hap - pier, she was afraid of losing him and reverting to how she had felt previously. The doctor emphasized to her that it was not the man, but her own body's ability to heal that did the healing. But afraid she still was! A few month passed and one day she came back in her old, sick condition. "He left me!"she said. And all the doctor's reminders that the healing had come from within herself were again of no avail.

Many people are under the impression that health is not something we are born with, but something we have to achieve or to strive for. So they spend a good deal of their lives trying to "get" it. Doctors of all kinds and a variety of other healing professionals have offered many ways to "achieve" this "goal."

We long for health, expecting that the more we know and learn, the better we will get. Yet, the underlying conviction re - mains that "it is normal to be sick and life is a struggle," rather than "it is normal to be healthy and life is easy."

"It is one of the oddest experiences of my life as a physician to continually perform histories and physical examinations on persons, to do laboratory tests of various sorts, and then to counsel them on how to be healthier, only to be told, 'But I know that already.'"[1]

Regardless of the approach taken, symptom relief is the goal of most treatments. Yet, we find that symptoms usually return either in the same form or a different one. The attitude assumed is: "I am sick and I want to get well." This places the person in identity with the sickness, with that which is wrong.

I realized very quickly that if any changes were going to be made with Mary, this was the starting point: change or shift in

225

identity from what's wrong to what's right. "It takes a central switch in identity to let real change take place."[2]

We tend to find it easy to list what is wrong with ourselves, but we'd be hard-pressed to list what is right. We may start with family, friends and associates, move on to education and our past, and end up with our physical shape and conditioning. We may even describe compassion and deep feelings, but it would be evident that our identity would be wrapped up in externals. In other words, everything that we would say is based on what's outside of us – "...'I am sick' (with our minds), 'I am confused' (with our emotions), 'I am elated' or 'I am worried.' However, true identification is with life itself. 'I am life,' expressing through my body, mind and emotions."[3]

"It is not a case of changing external forms (the body for example); the forms are only a reflection of our con - sciousness. It's like trying to comb you hair while looking in the mirror, but combing the reflection instead! It is rather, allowing our consciousness to change, and the first step toward this is to recognize the state of consciousness we've been in."[4]

I asked Mary to list her background and, sure enough, it all came out! "I am fat, ugly, angry and upset. I hate my husband and my back and neck hurts." When it came to listing what was right she said, "I don't know; nothing seems to be right!" Her identity was wrapped up in everything around her, changing like a chameleon depending on the circumstances in which she found herself. I asked her if she ever considered that what she *is* has nothing to do with how she feels or what's happening external to her. She replied, "How else could you define yourself if not by this?"

I indicated to her that she was inherently perfect and beauti - ful, containing the qualities of love, compassion and trustworthi - ness, to name only a few. If change was to take place in her, the first step would be to acknowledge this. "What do you mean 'I am perfect and beautiful?'"she replied, with a tone of wonder and curiosity, "I'm fat, down-trodden and ugly!"

I am not suggesting that we deny the facts of physical symp - toms and feelings. Although we acknowledge these factors as being present, they are not 'who we are.' The tendency is to acknowledge their presence and then try to change them. It is impossible to change what's wrong to right: wrong is wrong and right is right!

By this time Mary and I had begun to develop a trusting relationship and even though she didn't accept what I had to say consciously, it seemed to me that at some level the message was getting through. And she kept coming back. I had previously ex - amined and x-rayed her and noted numerous positive findings, so I had good reason to bring her back.

As our identity begins to shift from the external to the internal (life), so does our experience. In Mary's case, she began to smile and laugh, even though she hadn't lost any weight. She seemed lighter and eager. Although her external environment was still the same, her internal environment was changing. Her symptoms hadn't changed and this was a dis - couraging factor, but I counseled her to be patient. "I don't know why I'm doing this, but somehow I trust you and it even seems that this might work." She must have said this to me at least 2-3 times per visit.

I continued to work with Mary, sometimes seeing her three times a week, always emphasizing these two areas: patience and trust. After a while she began to see visible results, which reinforced our movement together.

How do you tell a person that their pain may not go away immediately, that they may have some discomfort, and that I (the doctor) don't know how long it will take, and at the same time have them stay around? The answer is to encourage patience and trust.

At this point Mary had acknowledged where she had been, and begun to make a shift from an identity in externals to one in internals, and she had begun to discover that there are certain rhythms or pulsations to this shift as well. One day she said, "Alan, nothing is happening; I'm not better, my pain is still present, I feel like the same things are happening to me as before, yet for two weeks I felt so good!" I indicated to Mary that she just needed to be patient and not judge where she was at: "In all probability, one day you will wake up and it will be like the pain was never there." On her next visit, she reported that this was exactly what had happened.

It has been our habit to judge a process as not being right when we aren't comfortable with it, or when things just don't go the way we think they should. What we are in essence doing is preventing that process or cycle from completing itself, which creates further complications and problems. One example of this is the way we treat fever. Fever is the body's way of destroying toxins. When we take an aspirin to eliminate fever and create a feeling of comfort, we interfere with that process. And then we're surprised when the fever comes back again, or another symptom manifests.

So, Mary had seen, if only cursorily, that there was a process which she had an opportunity to facilitate, rather than stop or manipulate. She had begun to see that her previous experience was not permanent, but could change as she chang - ed. Mary had begun to have a new experience! How exciting it is to begin to recognize this, to gain a glimpse of freedom from the bounds and trappings of a previous identity.

"I am responsible for how I feel." It was great to see Mary begin to take on the role of being in command, responsible for the quality of her experience. From this perspective she began to take action to correct the life patterns which had long been out of alignment. She began enjoying being with her husband (and he hadn't changed!). She began to swim, lose weight, eat less, and choose more wholesome foods. She was uncharacteristically calm and at ease, open and joyful. She even began to exercise.

Yet, she would often say to me, "I am afraid that I may lose this!" The process up to this point had proceeded smoothly, but her concern was a very real one, for I knew that, in one sense, she was living off of me, and if she truly was to have a more permanent experience of wellness it was imperative that she deeply believe that it could all happen under her own steam.

Mary, like many other people, tended to be very hard on herself, and her criticism of others stemmed from self-judgement and frustration at her inability to effect change. Yet, before we can accept others we must truly accept ourselves. To my delight, Mary began to have this experience, which can be characterized as one of 'for-give-ness' both of herself and of others.

"I am not a failure! I am a focus of creative spirit in my world!" It is this change of identity in each moment that does the trick. Yes, occasional apologies and corrections are necessary, but even when we slip, how refreshing it is to make light of it and quickly re-establish our alignment with the nobility of our true character. Mulling over a mistake prolongs it. "Let go and live!"[5]

Mary began to communicate her enthusiasm and excitement to others. She began to find new ways of assisting her kids at school, and new ways of relating to other staff members.

I recall the saying by John Kennedy: "Ask not what you country can do for you, but what you can do for your country." Mary's orientation up to this point was still, "What can life do for me?" and I would be remiss not to mention that many people get to this point and think that they've "made it to the top," only to fall again, this time harder and further. If the approach is still, "How can I *get* better? How can I *get* help? What can I do to feel better?" the end result will be the same old thing – temporary change, and no more.

This is where the ultimate shift takes place. In chiropractic we call it the "Big Idea." The question posed is, "What will life have me do in this moment?" The life that I am utilizes the facilities of body, mind and heart for its expression, and if I am one with it in *every* single moment, I am truly giving up an old identity for one that is totally new.

It is from this perspective that ongoing health is known. It is not something that needs to be strived for or attained. It is some - thing that already is. "Health is the unhindered expression of life moving through the body, mind and heart."[6] This *is* the "heart of healing."

Today Mary comes across as alert, vivacious and fully alive. She continues to discover and move with the rhythms and pulsations of life. No longer my patient, she is now my friend.

The wonder of life is there to be explored. And when healer and patient join together in life's process, they can explore it together.

**Notes:**

1 Larry Dossey, *Beyond Illness,* Shambhala Publications, Boston, p. 68.
2 Larry Krantz, M. D., "The Essential Change" *Healing Currents,* Vol. 6, No. 5.
3 Bill Wilkinson, "Attunement With Life" Seminar, Vol. 2: Orientation.
4 William Bahan, D.C., "Alignment With Life," *Healing Currents,* Vol. 6, No. 4.
5 Bill Wilkinson, "Attunement With Life" Seminar, Vol. 5: Forgiveness
6 Taken from a speech by Bill Bahan, D.C.

# The Invisible Healer

## by Bill Bahan

We can never find agreement in beliefs. Any disagreement that we find anywhere, whether it is in the healing arts or in the political situation, is because of a conflict between beliefs. Beliefs will vary, but life is one. When there are those who begin to find a centering in life they find oneness, and they begin to find that all the problems they had at the base were consequent upon not maintaining that agreement in life. If life is great enough to maintain our cosmos, I'm sure it's great enough to correct ill physical conditions.

\*\*\*

Whether it is the need for physical healing or the need for healing of conflicts between nations, as long as man keeps ignoring the invisible realm of his being and gets all centered in the external environment and all the things that are going on around him, well, there is no hope. But as there are those who begin to recognize that the true value is in this invisible realm, and keep it right and clear and wholesome, then nobility of character will begin to reflect itself in the visible realm.

\*\*\*

*Bill Bahan, D.C. was the founding director of the Whole Health Institute. He graduated from Palmer School of Chiropractic in 1949, and developed an extremely successful practice in Derry, New Hampshire, charging no fees but allowing each patient to pay within his or her means. Bill's later years were devoted to lecturing in North America and internationally, pioneering the importance of attitude and spirit in healing. He died in 1983; his last words summarized his life: "Let love radiate." This chapter is a collection of quotes from his extemporaneous talks.*

We know that there is a difference between a corpse and a live person. A corpse, we would say is minus the invisible realm. This invisible aspect of our being has very definite qualities. If we identify with qualities that are not true to the nature of this invisible aspect of being, we'll put wrong causes into motion, which will bring forth ill effects.

The word *doctor* means *teacher;* the true doctor is the one who gets down to the nuts and bolts of the situation and explains to the person where his basic problem is. If the person just wants a patch-up job, well, that's all right: we can use all these techniques that offer some relief. But if both the doctor and the patient are really concerned with healing then we need to go to where the area of cause is, this invisible realm.

***

There are very definite personality traits, for instance, that you find in cancer patients. Perhaps I could mention certain traits noted in a lecture entitled "Management of the Emotional Aspects of Malignancy," by Dr. O. Carl Simonton, given at the University of Florida in Gainesville:

1) a great tendency to hold resentment and a marked inability to forgive;
2) a tendency towards self-pity;
3) a poor ability to develop and maintain meaningful, long-term relationships;
4) a very poor self-image.

This could include lots of people! Recently I was working with a woman who fit this whole pattern. The personality traits were there, but as yet there were no observable physical manifestations of any malignancy in her body. One could say that if she maintains that personality, the cancerous condition could show up. But the point is to assist her *now* – to assist her to allow this particular character that she has been portraying to change, because there is a true character present. As long as she has that invisible realm present with her she can begin to accept and to express that rather than continue to identify herself with this personality which is predisposed toward malignancy.

*** 

The physician's belief system parallels the belief system of the patient, and the traditional doctor-patient relationship reinforces this particular belief system; the doctor becomes involved in the distorted pattern that is showing in the patient. On the other hand, when the physician isn't wrapped up in the physical manifestation, he can look at the illness with serenity and see through it into the realm of cause. Many times he can't speak directly to the person he's working with, because it is something that one must approach delicately. But because of his own experience, having a clear inner realm within himself, he is able to project something – we might call it secret service – which is able to penetrate into the invisible realm of this person and offer a soothing, healing influence.

*** 

You can see again the need for the doctor to be the teacher, because if you say to the average person, "You need to take responsibility for this ill condition," they don't know how. What constitutes responsibility? You are responsible for the quality of spirit you express, and there can be no healing unless this changes. When it is a quality which is true to the truth, then there can be healing. People want healing, physical healing, mental or emotional healing, and they want to maintain these wrong qualities of spirit. But there is *no* healing without the expression of the right quality of spirit.

235

\*\*\*

People are finding that what they have thought themselves to be quickly cracks under a little bit of pressure. The imaginary self, which is a very thin veneer, doesn't have much survival value, but there is a true self which transcends that imaginary self. It is the self we should have learned to express as children, but we didn't. We were programmed into the imaginary self, but the true self is there or we couldn't have the imaginary self. If the true self isn't there the imaginary self isn't either. So we need to learn how to come through this imaginary self and not uphold it and defend it anymore. The truth needs no defense.

\*\*\*

So, how do we let this true self come out? First of all, we stop blaming things. Blame no one. We accept our circumstances exactly as they are. What would you think of a person whose hair was all messed up, and when he looked in the mirror he tried to straighten his hair in the reflected image? The image in the mirror is but a reflection of what is standing before the mirror. The whole world has been seeking to change the reflection, trying to manipulate and change the environment. As long as we do that, of course, things only become worse. As an individual, the image in the mirror is a reflection of what is going on in you. If you have a circumstance that you don't like and you think that circumstance should be different, you are just rebelling against your own reflection. Now doesn't it seem logical that rather than continuing the stupidity of trying to change the reflection in the mirror, we let some changes occur here, in number one, in *me*? The reflection immediately changes when I straighten my hair. Something is going on within myself and my environment is beginning to change. I'm no longer trying to change my environment.

\*\*\*

If our consciousness is full of the qualities of the true self, such as joy, that is intensified. Many of us expect that joy is going to come from the environment, but we can't get joy from "out there." If you *experience* joy it is because you *express* joy. Sometimes people inadvertently express it and when they express it they usually translate it as, "I'm having this experience because of my environment." Well, that isn't the case at all. If you know joy it's because you express joy. If your consciousness is filled with the qualities of your true self – joy, happiness, assurance, forgiveness – and you give these expression, they are what you will know.

\*\*\*

Now when people touch this realm of reality and then lose the experience of it, it's because they didn't know how to protect it. And when they lose it, they reminisce about "that time back there," because they've associated it with a particular place where they were at the time they touched it. "It was in Rocky Mountain National Park. What a great spot. That's where I had a wonderful experience." But it wasn't Rocky Mountain National Park. You just happened to be there, and while you were there you touched it, it was just the conception. You didn't realize what it was, but you felt it and it felt wonderful, and your mind translated it and said, "Heaven is in Rocky Mountain National Park. If I could only get back there again, that would be paradise." That's why people, when they have had such an experience, are always looking back to the time and place where it occurred, because they think it was the spot. But it wasn't. It was something which transpired within themselves.

\*\*\*

*Bill Bahan*

Is there hope for all the world? It all depends upon me, just me, and it doesn't matter where I happen to be. Each one can say this. The world needs people who share this state of consciousness. This world, which is our world, is our responsibility. We have been hostages of the imaginary self. There is no need of saying, "I can't help it." The imaginary self can pass away when we stop giving it our life energy, when we stop trying to uphold it. The moment we are honest with ourselves, recognizing that life is present in us, that we are here to express life's true qualities, and we *do* that, our world will begin to change.

I think it's a delightful time to be alive. This earth belongs to the Creator, and we are here to return it to Him. It was our decision to come. For this cause we came into the world. With that state of consciousness I don't think there is any circumstance or situation that is going to stop us.

# The Whole Health Institute

**Purpose:**
The Whole Health Institute (WHI) is a network of men and women actively participating in the healing arts. WHI is concerned with whole-person health care and the causes of health, and with extending a healing influence into the world. International in scope, this body is composed of health professionals and lay people whose interest in the healing pro - cess includes and transcends the basic mechanics of health care.

**Structure:**
The Whole Health Institute is a non-profit organization, guided by a Board of Directors and has as its resource an International Board of Advisors. The Institute sponsors a wide range of gatherings around the world. Through seminars and workshops, publications and audio tapes WHI presents the perspectives of many highly respected authorities in the healing arts.

**Membership:**
Membership is open to anyone who identifies with the spirit and purposes of the Whole Health Institute.WHI provides a point of connection and contact between like-minded people in their own locality and throughout the world.

There is no set price to join the Whole Health Institute, although it is suggested that donations be no less than $16 per year, which is the basic cost of processing a membership.

Included in membership is a one year subscription to *Healing Currrents,* the journal of the Whole Health Institute. Donations are tax deductible. One year subscriptions to *Healing Currents* are available for $16 in the United States, and $12 in US funds for those living outside of the U.S.

**For further information contact:**
Administrator, Whole Health Institute, 4817 N. County Rd. 29, Loveland, CO 80537 USA.

# Order Form

| Author, *Title,* Price: | | Number of Copies | Total |
|---|---|---|---|
| **Michael Burghley** | | | |
| *The Rising Tide of Change* | $5.95 | | |
| **Church and Sherr** | | | |
| *The Heart of the Healer* | $14.95 | | |
| **Norman Cousins** | | | |
| *The Healing Heart* | $13.95 | | |
| *Albert Schweitzer's Mission* | $16.95 | | |
| **Larry Dossey** | | | |
| *Space, Time and Medicine* | $14.95 | | |
| *Beyond Illness* | $9.95 | | |
| **Frances Horn** | | | |
| *I Want One Thing* | $7.50 | | |
| **Francis MacNutt** | | | |
| *Healing* | $9.95 | | |
| *The Power to Heal* | $12.95 | | |
| **Richard Moss** | | | |
| *The Black Butterfly* | $9.95 | | |
| *The I That Is We* | $8.95 | | |
| **Bernie Siegel** | | | |
| *Love, Medicine, & Miracles* Book | $17.45 | | |
| *Tapes* (set of 4) | $29.95 | | |
| **Andrew Vidich** | | | |
| *Healing into Life* (tape) | $7.95 | | |
| **Bill Wilkinson** | | | |
| *Attunement With Life* | $5.95 | | |
| **Subtotal** | | | |
| NY residents add 8.25% sales tax | | | |
| Shipping (see rates below) | | | |
| **Total** (Check or money order to Aslan Publishing) | | | |

**Shipping:** *Book Rate:* $1.50 first item, .50 each add item, 5 or more items free. (Allow 4-6 weeks for delivery.)
*First Class or UPS 2 day:* $3.50 first item, $1.00 each add item No C.O.D.'s. Satisfaction guaranteed.

**Mail to:** Aslan Publishing, Box 496-J, New York, NY 10032

240

# Reader Response Form

The two way flow of communication among healers is a source of inspiration and stimulation to the whole healing community. The editors would feel priviledged to receive feedback from readers about their response to this book and about similar experiences they may have had. So we invite you to use this page, or any other format, to enrich our understanding of the healing process of which we are all a part, and to assist us in preparing future material.

## Comments:

I felt the following chapters were particularly useful:

_____

_____

In future editions of this book, I would recommend the following changes:

Emphasize: _____

De-emphasize: _____

I have had some experiences similar to those you describe: (please use another page if necessary)_____

_____

_____

A crucial point in my growth as a healer was: _____

_____

_____

I would recommend the following books to you:

Title:                          Author:                     Publisher:

_____

_____

_____

I obtained my copy of this book at: (check one)

__Bookshop:  Name _____ City_____

__Conference: Name _____ City_____

__Catalogue:  Name _____

__Gift     __ Other: _____

My name is: _____

My address is: _____

Please return to: Aslan Publishing, PO Box 496-Q, New York, NY 10032, USA, or Mickleton House, Mickleton, Gloucestershire GL55 6RY, England